Leila Aboulela

Leila Aboulela rose to prominence in the first decade of the 21st century for her novels, short stories, and radio plays that are anchored in a sensitive and complex exploration of ordinary Muslim women attempting to gain autonomy in a Western world that casts them as misfits. This biography explores Aboulela's childhood and youth in Khartoum, her difficult migration to Scotland, and her unusual journey to becoming a writer. Shringarpure underscores the connections between Aboulela's life and her writing, focusing on experiences that have been both an impetus and an inspiration—not only as topics for her fiction but also as forces that drew her toward finding her voice as a writer.

Aboulela is claimed by many literary universes; from Sudanese and Scottish literature to Muslim women's literature, African literature, and Black British writing. This book weaves together interviews and literary criticism, exploring key life events to assemble a vivid portrait of a unique Muslim woman writer from Sudan.

Bhakti Shringarpure is a writer and editor based in Paris. She is the author of *Cold War Assemblages: Decolonization to Digital* (2019) and co-author of *India's Imperial Formations: Cultural Perspectives* (2024). She is the editor of the *Decolonize That!* book series and the anthologies *Literary Sudans: An Anthology of Literature from Sudan and South Sudan* (2016), *Imagine Africa, Volume 3* (2017), *Mediterranean: Migrant Crossings* (2018), and *Insurgent Feminisms: Writing War* (2023). Shringarpure co-founded *Warscapes* magazine in 2011, which has since transitioned into the Radical Books Collective, an initiative that builds community and strengthens solidarities through conversations, events, and podcasts on culture and politics. She is a research associate at the Department of African Literature at the University of the Witwatersrand, Johannesburg.

Routledge African Writers: Intellectual Biographies, Literary Histories

Routledge African Writers: Intellectual Biographies, Literary Histories is a series of concise intellectual biographies of African writers.

These short books situate writers within the context of their entire bodies of work, within debates around their oeuvres, as well as within the larger historical contexts of their literary, political and regional affiliations. The series emphasises the interconnections between writers and their worlds, demonstrating how the emergence and consolidation of their literary lives is rooted in particular historical, psychological and social contexts.

The series aims to redefine and democratize current understandings of the African literary canon. To that end, we feature writers whose works together reflect the diversity of ideas, topics, languages, regions, and genres that make up African literature.

Combining original scholarly expertise and archival research with an accessible writing style, these books will be useful guides for researchers and students in the fields of African, postcolonial and World literature, as well as the interested general reader.

To submit proposals, please contact the series editors, or Routledge's African Studies Editor, Helena Hurd (helena.hurd@tandf.co.uk)

Series Editors:
Lily Saint, Wesleyan University, USA
Bhakti Shringarpure

1. Leila Aboulela
Writing as Refuge
Bhakti Shringarpure

Leila Aboulela

Writing as Refuge

Bhakti Shringarpure

Routledge
Taylor & Francis Group
LONDON AND NEW YORK

Designed cover image: ©Emily Maciness

First published 2027
by Routledge
4 Park Square, Milton Park, Abingdon, Oxon OX14 4RN

and by Routledge
605 Third Avenue, New York, NY 10158

Routledge is an imprint of the Taylor & Francis Group, an informa business

British Library Cataloguing-in-Publication Data
A catalogue record for this book is available from the British Library

ISBN: 9781032307985 (hbk)
ISBN: 9781032307992 (pbk)
ISBN: 9781003306719 (ebk)

DOI: 10.4324/9781003306719

Typeset in Galliard
by KnowledgeWorks Global Ltd.

Contents

List of Figures

Introduction

Leila Aboulela

"I remember being a child in a garden in Sudan."

Almost six decades later, Leila's first memory is a lush and sensory one. The blinding brightness of the afternoon is ebbing. The garden is very green. Someone is watering the plants, and the aroma of moist soil wafts through the air. Perhaps this is the house in Khartoum's Al-Amarat neighborhood where Leila spent her childhood. But it might be in Wad Madani, a town on the banks of the Blue Nile, southeast of Khartoum, where Leila's Egyptian grandparents had taken up temporary residence.

The exact location does not matter because the imagery, the fragrance and the feeling of being warmly cared for evoke something quintessentially Sudanese for Leila. The image of teenager Mahmud Khalifa stands out in Leila's mind. Mahmud, her mother's younger brother who was just ten years older than Leila, was a kind and indulgent playmate to the two-and-a-half-year-old girl.

While family members and granular depictions of life in Sudan are a wellspring of inspiration for Leila's fiction, Leila's stories appear to be spurred by her experience of migration from Sudan—her warm place of home—to the cold alienation of Scotland. There is a cruelty with which she administers the fates of her characters. Beautiful and precious real-life memories are twisted, ruptured, and reframed in order to deprive them of the warmth of remembrance, and allow her women protagonists to experience a saturated kind of mourning, one that stems from displacement and dislocation.

Home was forever fixed as Sudan. But eventually, perhaps grudgingly, she would come to call Scotland home too. Over time, Leila's large oeuvre of writing would come to span many worlds and many temporalities—including bringing together Sudan and Scotland, two very different landscapes and histories, into a unique narrative tapestry. But she would always seek the elusive feeling of a vivid first memory of

DOI: 10.4324/9781003306719-1

Figure 0.1 Leila Aboulela, age 2, garden

that happy afternoon, the intimacy of being in the fold of family and the Sudanese way of life.

***

A steady ascent into the literary world

Leila Aboulela rose to prominence in the first decade of the 21st century. Her novels, short stories, and radio plays are anchored in a sensitive and complex exploration of ordinary Muslim women who are often building their lives and gaining autonomy in a Western world that casts them as misfits.

She was born in 1964 in Cairo to an Egyptian mother, Mona Khalifa, and Sudanese father, Fuad Aboulela, and spent her childhood and youth in Khartoum, Sudan. However, she has lived most of her adult life outside of Sudan, in Aberdeen, Scotland, where her husband, Nadir Mahjoub's career trajectory in the petroleum industry took them. Nadir's career has also meant that she has made a home for short periods of time in London, Jakarta, Abu Dhabi, Dubai, and Doha.

Leila's ascent in the literary world has been steady, with a new publication every few years, and a tactfully resistant and much-admired literary persona. She is claimed by many literary universes—from Sudanese and Scottish literature to Muslim women's literature, as well as African literature, and Black British writing. Her books do the work of bridging the often-strained cultural, linguistic, and geopolitical relations between a mainly Muslim and ethnically and linguistically Arab region of the Middle East and North Africa, and the vast, predominantly Black region of sub-Saharan Africa. Furthermore, Leila has also been writing about and from Scotland, thus adding yet another dimension to her preoccupation with places on the margins of empire.

Her own life experiences have been impetus and inspiration—not simply as topics for her fiction, but as forces that drew her *a priori* to finding her voice as a writer. In the late nineties, Leila found herself isolated and unmoored in London with a small baby to care for, while Nadir was away for long periods on oil rigs. Eventually they moved to Aberdeen, and here, she was drawn into the world of reading and writing after signing up for a correspondence course in creative writing on a whim. Always a voracious reader, the course-assigned reading lists opened up worlds of women's writers, Black writers, British writers, and postcolonial writers, and armed Leila with a language to express the journey of migration, motherhood, and faith that she was on. "In the greyness of culture shock and bad weather, the writing was there, warm and glowing, a new hope, an opportunity, a way of contact with my past," she explains.[1] Writing became a refuge and a balm. This period of coming into being as a writer was also one of finding her place as a migrant Muslim woman in Western society, and the two became irrevocably entangled.

Leila started by writing and publishing short stories in small Scottish venues. She went on to publish her first novel, *The Translator,* in 1999, for a small Scottish press, and this was followed by *Minaret* in 2005, which received a far wider reception. Both novels comprise beautifully drawn, unsparing portraits of women protagonists who often suffer from an inferiority complex and find refuge in religion. These women are not particularly good-looking, nor exceptional in terms of intellect or careers; their triumphs, if any, are predicated upon a kind of self-reconciliation, and an acceptance of circumstances played out in a minor key of the novel's universe. In these novels, Leila has crafted a complex female interiority grounded in faith and religious practice, etched against the backdrop of a hostile West.

Her next two works, *Lyrics Alley* (2010) and *The Kindness of Enemies* (2015), were historical novels, and with the latter, Leila's political leanings and defense of Islam and Muslims came to the fore. Her following novel, *Bird Summons* (2019), returned to the topic of Muslim women navigating life in Scotland. Most recently, *River Spirit* (2023) fictionalized political events in 19th-century Sudan. Along the way, she has also produced two short-story collections, *Coloured Lights* (2001) and *Elsewhere, Home* (2018), a novella, *A New Year* (2025), and over a dozen radio plays.

Leila's journey from a timid migrant mother to a unique literary voice was surprising, but it was not necessarily long or arduous. It has unfolded within two synchronous phenomena: the ascent of African literature in the Anglophone realm, and the rise of anti-Muslim hatred globally after September 11, 2001.

Leila became the first recipient of the Caine Prize for African Writing for her short story "The Museum" in the year 2000. The Caine Prize ushered in a new era for Anglophone writing from and about the African continent. These publishing circuits tended to originate from the UK and, to some extent, North America, privileged diaspora perspectives, and popularized the theme of migration in African literature. Leila's work and life trajectory fit perfectly within this wave in publishing, and boosted her profile.

Despite the prize and steady publications, Leila was relatively unknown outside of Scotland. She was on a lone journey in her attempt to depict the lives of Muslim women in the UK, and to engage with prejudice against Islam. However, her novel *Minaret* gained traction in a post-9/11 climate and the ensuing War on Terror. This was partially because it offered an insider view into Muslim lives, and partially because it resonated as an exposé of Islamophobia in the Western world.

Since then, Leila has come to occupy a peculiar place; on the one hand, she is deemed as conservative and anti-secular, but on the other hand, it has also become hard to shake off the sheer level of political critique her work has mounted against an anti-Muslim West.

Some of these paradoxes were resolved in 2025 when she was awarded the PEN Pinter Prize in London. This is a prize given to a writer who "casts an 'unflinching, unswerving' gaze upon the world, and shows a 'fierce intellectual determination…to define the real truth of our lives and our societies'."[2] Leila was given this award for engaging with the lives of Muslim, migrant women against the backdrop of unending wars in Sudan and Palestine, and the rise of Islamophobia worldwide.

On the biography

I first encountered Leila Aboulela's work through her novel *Minaret* almost five or six years after it had been published. As someone who had been living in New York in the aftermath of 9/11, I often experienced discrimination because I was perceived as Muslim, and *Minaret* spoke directly to everything that was happening around me. The psychic and material violence of the War on Terror proliferated in all aspects of our lives: educational institutions, travel, border and visa regimes, media narratives, as well as conversations and interpersonal relationships. Reading *Minaret* validated the idea that the West indeed had a real animus toward Muslims. And *Minaret* offered a language for the uneven and difficult effects that these structural biases can have on women, in particular.

As I became familiar with all of Leila's work, I realized that though her novels were popular with Muslims and the Muslim diaspora population, her work was received with ambivalence by Western readers. For this demographic, Leila's faith-based writing and embrace of Islam were incompatible with her interest in women's stories. The rise of compulsory secularism within mainstream liberal discourses often views Christian values, culture, and signifiers as universal and others' Islam and Muslims, in particular. Through her books, interviews, and stories, Leila has mounted a gentle but firm critique of this Christian-centric approach to literature and has pushed readers and critics to investigate their own entrenched anti-Muslim reading practices. Within these narratives, Leila's women do not need to be rescued from Islam, but rather, they embrace their faith and move to find solutions, growth, and resolution *through* religion. The perception of a Muslim trajectory for women has been a sticking point for Western readerships, and Leila's women characters are not given credit for their self-reflexivity, empowerment, and acts of transgression. It is Leila's resistance to the bulwark of the West's embedded coloniality and Christianity, always framed as secular, that I find admirable.

Leila's writing is also important to me because of its ability to reframe the representation of Sudan within Anglophone readerships. On the one hand, a stubborn, unchanging canon of African literature had deemed Tayeb Salih as the sole voice from Sudan, and comparisons between her and Salih were constant when Leila first began writing. Even though Leila is influenced by Salih, the two writers are very different. Salih, though seen as progressive in his outlook on women, creates distinctly masculine worlds, and his Sudan is primarily rural. Leila's writing is dedicated, at its core, to questions of gender and women's worlds, and she also tends to write city novels whether the location is Khartoum, London, Cairo, or Aberdeen. Leila's work departs from Salih in several ways, and it offers an updated prism to understand Sudan.

In the last few decades, Sudan has come to be synonymous with war and dictatorship. In fact, my own interest in and engagement with Sudan was due to the *longue durée* war in Darfur. When I had the opportunity to publish an anthology of fiction from Sudan and South Sudan in 2013, I reached out to Leila and solicited her help in locating younger writers. She had been giving workshops and offering support to writers who were narrating war and displacement. Yet, war was not a theme in Leila's work, at least not until her recent historical novel, *River Spirit.* Contemporary discourses about Sudan could not get past the stereotype of wretchedness: violence, poverty, tyranny, war, and hunger. Writers like Binyavanga Wainana had warned that the Western, white, and colonial gaze pathologized Africa through these fixed frames of negative representation.[3] Leila's nostalgic gaze toward Sudan offers a welcome respite from a preoccupation with abject imagery and themes. In many of her works, Khartoum is brought to life as a vibrant city, thus functioning as an antidote to singular representations of Sudan.

Choosing Leila as a subject of biography automatically ensures that these same gaps are addressed and explored, and the book thus becomes an inadvertent intervention into several interwoven themes: mainstream knowledge about Sudan; the difficulties of migration; pervasive Islamophobia in the West, and the challenges faced by Muslim women. This biography explores Leila's life and writing chronologically and builds on events and experiences in her life that become foundational to her fiction. Leila's beloved Khartoum is brought to life, as is her mission to defend Muslim women through storytelling.

The book begins with the history of her family–the Sudanese Aboulelas from her father's side, and the Egyptian Khalifas from her mother's side; worlds, memories, and tensions that Leila navigates repeatedly in her work. It then proceeds to encapsulate Leila's girlhood years in Khartoum, while exploring her relationship with her mother, a vital and complex bond that Leila excavates in many of her works. Falling in love and marrying Nadir is a pivotal moment in Leila's life, and many of her novels often feature love and marriage plots. However, after getting married, Leila's life takes a drastic turn when Nadir's job leads to a traumatic voyage away from her beloved Khartoum. Life in London and in Aberdeen has long-lasting effects on Leila since a much-awaited return to Sudan is thwarted due to political instabilities in the country.

The second half of the biography focuses on Leila's foray into creative writing. All this time, Leila had been pursuing her MPhil in Statistics at the London School of Economics and had assumed that she would progress toward a PhD. Yet this trajectory was cut short abruptly when her supervisors informed her that they did not think she could advance to a PhD. Leila was shocked and humiliated, but unbeknownst to her at that time, she had also been liberated.

She signed up for a correspondence course in creative writing and has not looked back since. During this time, she also cultivated an exciting social world, primarily through a community of women in her local Aberdeen mosque.

Upon publication of her first novel and some short stories, Leila accepted that she had indeed become a writer. The final chapter offers a survey of Leila's three decades as a writer and the quixotic nature of acclaim for a Muslim woman writer in a post-9/11 world. Ever since Leila started writing in the early nineties, she has traversed an extraordinary and epic distance. This book illustrates that her journey as a writer was shaped by three intensely powerful forces that are a perennial source of pain but have also propelled her success: leaving Sudan but preserving and encapsulating it in her fiction; the simultaneously anchoring and unmooring influence of her mother, Mona; and her deeply evolved faith and defense of Islam and Muslims.

The book's research process comprised long interviews with Leila herself in addition to members of her family, friends and colleagues, email correspondence, and visits to Khartoum and Omdurman (July 2022), Toronto (May 2022), and to Edinburgh and Aberdeen (August to November 2022). The book also draws on the extensive body of published material about her: academic publications in literary studies, religious studies, and women's studies; articles in mainstream media; and media appearances over the years. The full list of references and a note on the citation method have been included at the end of the book. The biography has been stitched together through this plethora of material and attempts to construct a narrative of Leila's life as it intersects with her writing.

The biography is certainly not comprehensive. It is one of the first in a series of African writers' biographies meant to canonize, celebrate, and, in some cases, introduce them to students, researchers, and general readers. To that end, the book has been deliberately kept short and accessible. The goals of the book are manifold. For those unfamiliar with Leila's work, it offers an immersion into the world that created her and, in turn, the uniquely Sudanese and Scottish worlds that she created. For those familiar with her writing, the biography offers a necessary context given the sheer extent of how she is misunderstood for being an unabashedly Muslim writer, and for giving space to religious Muslim women in her fiction.

This book was born of its inspiring subject: Leila Aboulela. I am grateful to Leila for her sensitive, passionate, and unwavering commitment to representing one of the most maligned groups of people today: Muslim women. I am also moved and spurred by her stubborn insistence on Muslim worldmaking within an Anglophone literary culture that continually rejects it. It was Leila's calm yet steely resistance along with my desire to bring myself closer to Sudan that led me to take on this endeavor.

Working on this biography has been deeply rewarding and a source of great pleasure. Every phase of the research has uncovered new layers of Leila's personality, character, creativity, and intellect. In contrast, this immersion into the individual has also revealed large gaps in studies of Sudanese literary history, Muslim women, anti-Muslim reading practices in English literary studies, and the place and politics of Muslims and Islam in the world today. I hope this book will provide a counter-narrative but also a map for understanding her life and writing, and will serve as an invitation for researchers to tackle these marginalized areas of study and broaden the world's understanding of these topics.

–Bhakti Shringarpure (December 2025)

Notes

1 Leila Aboulela, "Moving Away from Accuracy," *Alif: Journal of Comparative Poetics*, no. 22 (2002), 204.
2 Harold Pinter, "Art, Truth & Politics" (Nobel Lecture, Stockholm, December 7, 2005), The Nobel Prize, https://www.nobelprize.org/prizes/literature/2005/pinter/lecture/
3 Binyavanga Wainaina, "How to Write About Africa," *Granta*, no. 92 (Winter 2005), https://granta.com/how-to-write-about-africa/

1 Settling Sudan

An Egyptian Story

"I think part of the grieving that I went through when I left Sudan was a kind of guilt that I was not close enough to my Sudanese side."

Leila moved to London with her one-year-old son Kareem to start a master's degree in Statistics while her husband Nadir was posted on an oil rig. The plan was to return to Sudan once Nadir found a different job and once she finished her degree, but once Leila realized that would no longer be the case—for a variety of political reasons—she blamed herself for not fully connecting with the Sudanese side of her identity when she did live there. But this was not Leila's fault. She may have grown up in Sudan's vibrant capital, Khartoum, but she had been conditioned into a ubiquitous Egyptianness.

Born to an Egyptian mother, Mona Khalifa, from Cairo, and a Sudanese father, Fuad Aboulela, whose family had arrived from Esna in southern Egypt to Sudan over two generations ago, Egypt was omnipresent in Leila's Sudanese life. And due to Egypt's colonial history with Sudan, these two strands of Leila's identity exist in an uneasy alliance.

The Aboulela family came to Sudan at a time when borders were not strictly demarcated. They carried with them a proud sense of belonging to Egypt even as they fell in love with Sudan. Hasanain Aboulela—Leila's great-grandfather—was the first known ancestor to ride in from Esna along with his brother Mahmoud sometime in the mid-1880s.

Over time, the Aboulelas not only made a home in Sudan, but they settled in, in the true sense of the word. Persevering, tireless, and gifted with immense business acumen, they not only grew their own agricultural transport business but also expanded the colonial and post-colonial agricultural, engineering, and commerce sectors in Sudan, thus becoming one of the wealthiest and most prominent families in the country. By the time Leila was born in 1964, her grandfather Mustafa Aboulela had built a saraya, a small family mansion, in Omdurman. His many offspring had received the best education in Egypt, were the first to own cars, and had dedicated themselves to various aspects of the still-thriving family business.

DOI: 10.4324/9781003306719-2

The Aboulelas did not doubt that they were Sudanese, and years of intermarriage had altered the ethnic and racial fabric of the family. But the many decades of Egyptian colonial rule in Sudan, pride in an Egyptian lineage, and the constant back-and-forth between the two countries meant that a sense of Egyptian cultural superiority was also embedded in the Aboulela family.

Fuad further consolidated this connection when he married Mona from Cairo, who marked herself as different in the teeming Sudanese household. Academically ambitious and living the modern life of a nuclear family in Khartoum, Mona showed little patience for traditional Sudanese conventions and often tired of the large weekly gatherings at the saraya. At home, they ate Egyptian food, and Leila even wore clothes bought in Cairo. Leila recalls lively lunchtime debates between Mona and Fuad about differences between Sudan and Egypt. "I began to realize what was going on at home, that there was a kind of Egyptian colonialism."

After Leila began attending the University of Khartoum, the years of unconscious Egyptianness began to come undone. Students came from all over the country to gain a prestigious education in the country's capital, and Leila found herself attracted to a different Sudan; perhaps a provincial, less urban, and more pastoral Sudan that she was only becoming aware of.

Soon after her time at the university, Leila would be flung out of Sudan and into the melancholy of London and Aberdeen. She would come to feel guilty of having left without immersing herself in her Sudanese side.

It would take her a long time, but she would come to rectify this gap in her writing. She would return and reconnect. She would unearth the history of her family in her third novel *Lyrics Alley,* and again in her sixth novel *River Spirit.*

Not only would she uphold a romantic and nostalgic version of Omdurman and the Aboulela family in *Lyrics Alley,* but she would also expose and critique the Egyptian superiority that she began to understand as a type of colonial influence.

***

From Esna to Omdurman

> "Omdurman was a labyrinth of alleys, houses built from rammed earth. Zamzam walked back through a town that was beginning to bloom as a new capital in an independent state. Emigrants pouring in, the families and tribes of those who had borne the ravages of this war, who had paid the prices for victory...It was heaving hot with hopes, heady with tomorrow. A town confident in its foundation, ready to be built."[1]
>
> —Zamzam in *River Spirit.*

In *Lyrics Alley* and *River Spirit*, Leila has painstakingly and lovingly sketched out Omdurman, a city that is not only of great historical importance in Sudan but also one that has deep personal resonances for the Aboulela family. Nestled on the west bank of the River Nile, a mere 20 minutes by car across the bridge from the capital Khartoum, Omdurman has no rush hour traffic or disturbances and blockages caused by the political disruptions of the past decade.

The story of the patriarch who traveled 1500 or so kilometers south from Esna to Omdurman in 1885 is remembered and orally transmitted today with ease and pride by various members of the Aboulela clan. Hasanain Aboulela arrived in Omdurman at the behest of a fellow Egyptian from Esna—a man named Hassan Bey Abdelmonium, a high-ranking official in Khartoum's Ottoman administration, who was married to a Sudanese woman, herself the daughter of a landowning mother and a Moroccan soldier in the Ottoman army. Leila details the "charming" backstory to this journey, namely the summoning of Hasanain during the Mahdist War, which raged from 1881 to 1899 and profoundly altered the shape of Sudan.

The ascent of the "Expected Mahdi," the 40-year-old Sufi leader Muhammed Ahmed ibn Abdallah, who united various Sudanese groups under the banner of Islam by convincingly claiming that the Prophet had chosen him to liberate Sudan from over six decades of corrupt and unjust Turkish and Egyptian rule, began at Aba Island, 150 miles south of Khartoum in 1881. Ismail Pasha, the Khedive of Egypt had been ousted in 1879 by the Ottoman Sultan under pressure from the French and British governments, but as Turkish rule waned, the arrival of the British was imminent.[2]

River Spirit depicts this 18-year period of war, displacement, and turmoil from a diverse set of perspectives, in which historical figures such as the charismatic yet tyrannical Mahdi and the ambitious colonial General Charles George Gordon—who met his death in Sudan—mingle with fictional characters. Two characters in particular—woman Rabiha and devotee Musa—illustrate the Mahdi's influence upon the hearts and minds of the people.

As the uprising gained traction and the ousting of the Egyptian administration and Egyptians generally appeared inevitable, Abdelmoniem in Omdurman sought to marry off as many of his five "fair" daughters, lest they be dishonored by the Mahdist "hordes." Leila recounts the story thus: "At first fearing rape, they had the girls locked up in a cellar. Then when things calmed down, the girls were allowed out of the cellar—but still fearing pressurized marriages, the father (in a precarious position with regards to his livelihood and Ottoman status now that he was on the wrong side of the new rulers) wrote to his family [back] in Esna and begged for five "studs"[3] (his wording) to come and save his five daughters by marrying them."

Hasanain, a distant relative, was one of the "studs." He married Zeynab, and his brother Mahmoud married another one of the sisters. This is how the Egyptian Aboulelas of Esna came to settle in Sudan.

They made their home in Sudan at a time of immense upheaval and before the set demarcation of colonial borders. They started with small businesses and grew to own land and become instrumental in steering the agricultural sector in future years. Despite having Egyptian roots and the privileges associated with being Egyptian in the days of the condominium, the Aboulelas identified as Sudanese, due to their long history of affiliations between South Egypt and Northern Sudan. The Egyptians living in these areas had known foreign rule from parts of Africa, the Middle East and Europe for several generations, and were considered to have hybrid origins. They had inherited a hybrid way of life due to an influx of migration from Mauritania, Morocco, Tunisia, and Libya, and they also imbibed traditions from Yemen, Iraq, and Syria.

By 1885, Khartoum was officially in the hands of the Mahdists, and neighboring Omdurman was slowly growing as those displaced from the long and ongoing civil war began to sink roots into the city. As the 19th century was coming to a close, the original Mahdi had passed away in 1881, leaving the new Khalifa in charge. While he succeeded in developing Omdurman as a center, the Khalifa never managed to consolidate power across the large swathes of Sudanese territory, nor did he unite the many ethnic, linguistic, and geographically disparate groups in Sudan.

French and Italian interests in various parts of Sudan and the ongoing Mahdist war complicated British efforts to sustain their power in Egypt. General Horatio Herbert Kitchener was ordered to secure control of the Nile waters and to intervene to help Khedive Ismail of Egypt push back the Mahdists, who were still fighting against Egyptian rule. His strategy was to construct military railways to "secure his communications, transport large numbers of troops, vast quantities of arms and supplies, and even gunboats in sections."[4]

Taken by surprise by the Anglo-Egyptian incursion, the Khalifa and his army suffered a staggering defeat in Karary in 1898, a few miles north of Omdurman. The Khalifa retreated into the western countryside as Kitchener took over the battered palace in Khartoum. The British were officially in Sudan by 1899.

The Anglo-Egyptian Condominium deal mandated Britain and Egypt's shared sovereignty over Sudan. The 1898 agreement did not make Sudan part of the British Empire. A Governor-General, granted extraordinary civil and military powers, would be appointed by the Khedive on the recommendation of the British. The establishment of the condominium placed British civilian administrators on top, Egyptians at the middle level, and Sudanese at the lowest rung. Without doubt, the generation of Egyptians who settled Sudan during this time benefited tremendously from this hierarchy, and the Aboulelas were no different.

Over time, borders were demarcated through various agreements with Ethiopia, Uganda, and Belgian Congo. A few years later, Darfur, which had broken away from Egypt during the Mahdist wars in the 1890s, was also annexed to Sudan, and the Fur Sultanate was dissolved. The British also embarked on economic, social, and political development projects in the regions of Sudan that were considered strategic and beneficial to them. The British-initiated Gezira Scheme to irrigate the Gezira plains with the waters of the Blue Nile to produce long staple cotton would ensure the success and wealth of the Aboulela family for future generations to come.

Hasanain Aboulela and Sons

Hasanain did not arrive in Sudan with much to his name. Family members speculate that he may have traveled back and forth between Barbar, a village about 400 kilometers north of Khartoum, and Khartoum, since it was a strategic hub for conducting trade between Sudan and Egypt. Operating on a small scale, Hasanain's business started around 1901 and consisted primarily of exporting goods such as gum arabic, sesame, sorghum, and other crops native to Sudan.

Hasanain and Zeynab had four sons—Mohammed, Awad, Mustafa, and Mahmoud—all of whom dedicated themselves to the task of expanding "Hasanain Aboulela and Sons," their father's small agricultural business. The four sons showed a talent for business, and Hasanain Aboulela and Sons expanded rapidly under the leadership of the oldest son, the "mastermind," Mohammed.

As with many of the colonies, the coming of the British Empire meant the construction of railways. Kitchener's railway line might have been originally built for military purposes, but it propelled the opening of a "trade route from central Sudan through Egypt to the Mediterranean and beyond."[5] The patriarch Hasanain and his four sons were used to days of arduous travel on foot, by donkey, or by boats as they set up businesses in various parts of Sudan. But the coming of the train lines allowed them to set up business outposts in Cairo and in Khartoum, which was slowly recovering from the long war, bolstering their business and ambition.[6]

With railway connections to and from Khartoum to Port Sudan and to Egypt, and with the implementation of the Gezira Scheme leading to the construction of the Sennar dam, the cotton industry and agriculture began to boom. The Gezira plains are a large, triangle-shaped area of land nestled between the Blue and White Nile, measuring about 300,000 acres.

The Sennar Dam, which opened in 1926 after several years of construction, is an impressive and gigantic structure that operates on a gravity basis and allows almost the entire huge landmass to be irrigated. The scheme devoted one-third of this area to cotton and the remainder to food crops such as maize and lubia beans. The government railway was also laid across the dam, connecting Sennar to Khartoum and then extending farther north all the way up to Port Sudan.[7]

Hasanain Aboulela and Sons grew rapidly as the cotton industry—and agriculture, more broadly—thrived for those who were able to ally their commercial endeavors with the ambitions of the British and Egyptian entities. Soon, they started a Cairo office which was managed by the youngest brother Mahmud, who was in charge of receiving goods from his brothers in Sudan. The Aboulela presence in Egypt grew exponentially during the early decades of the 20th century, making it one of the very few flourishing Sudanese businesses in Egypt.

The older brothers, Mohammed and Awad, only had a rudimentary education at Quranic school; but the two younger brothers, Mustafa and Mahmoud, were likely exposed to more schooling and a life of travel from doing business in Egypt and Europe. Photos in the family archive point to the diversity of lifestyles and cultural influences almost too plainly, with the oldest brother, Mohammed, dressed in traditional loose-fitting clothing and a white turban, and Mahmoud, the youngest, in a pinstripe suit—but with a traditional skull cap as an accessory. Mahmoud had settled in Cairo and ran the family business from there.[8]

In Sudan, Mustafa Hasanain Aboulela was just as ambitious as his brothers, and active in furthering the family business. But he also embodied a deeply cosmopolitan mobility. He was married to Fatima, a distant cousin of Mauritanian heritage, and together they had ten children—five boys and five girls—the youngest of whom was Fuad, Leila's father. Fatima died young when Fuad was only a child, and Mustafa divided his time, spending half a year in Geneva, Switzerland, and the other half in Khartoum.

Suave and elegant with a taste for bespoke suits and expensive ties, Mustafa had a hotel suite reserved in his name all year round in Geneva, and "there was not a single night or meal that he would eat by himself," Mona recounts. While this may suggest an exciting bachelor lifestyle, family members who visited him recount that his social life revolved around work and expanding business networks, and there was no hint of romantic liaisons. He also remained keenly involved in his children's lives despite his time abroad, ensuring that his sons received their education at the best schools in Cairo and the UK. Sudan was still the epicenter of Mustafa's aspirations and imagination, and this culminated in him initiating and overseeing the construction of a grand saraya—a palatial two-story family home—in Omdurman.

Figure 1.1 Mustafa Aboulela (left) and Mohamed and Mahmoud Hasanain Aboulela (right)

Inaugurated in 1955 after several years of construction, the saraya included a majestic formal staircase, floors built out of Italian marble, and grounds that held a circular English fountain. The ceilings boasted impressive height and were supported by large marble pillars. A wrap-around terrace on the first floor with a formal balcony overlooking the grounds, and the spacious front patio completes the impression that this is, indeed, a palace. The back of the home carried over features of a traditional Sudanese homestead, with an open kitchen and courtyard.[9] Family members who lived there remember a bustling household where the formal front section and the busy back areas merged seamlessly, when pet ducks marched through the salon areas to reach the fountains in the garden.

Mustafa, now a patriarch with a large family of children, grandchildren, and a multitude of cousins, built his dream mansion during the heyday of Sudanese construction and architecture. The Atbara cement factory was set up in 1947 and began producing and selling high-quality cement.[10] Work on the saraya ended just in time, as the Anglo-Egyptian condominium came to an end in 1956, and a newly independent Sudan saw the beginning of political turmoil. Additionally, with the new British-designed capital, Khartoum, ready and replete with modernist architecture and urban planning, there came about a slow, steady movement of younger families out of joint family setups in Omdurman to single-family homes in Khartoum.

Omdurman kept its cultural currency as the main city in Sudan for several decades, even as war-ruined Khartoum was being strategically developed by the British as a capital in the first decades of the 20th century.

Figure 1.2 The Aboulela saraya owned by Umma party, July 2022, Omdurman

The Aboulelas were rooted in Omdurman and owned several homes inhabited by various joint family units; several of which have kept their old facades and interiors.

Unlike the spectacular and uniquely designed saraya, these homes are more traditionally Sudanese, one-story homes built in the populous heart of the city. Nestled among Omdurman's small, winding alleys, these homes were within walking distance of each other as well as to the bustling souk, now said to be one of the largest in Sudan. Aside from some simple, necessary renovations, these homes remain untouched by new gadgets or modern interior décor. Modest and boxy-looking on the outside, each house was bounded by a high mud or brick wall. The interiors were elegantly furnished with cool, patterned tiles and large bedrooms lined with up to five or six beds, unlike the hierarchical design of European-style spaces, where the best rooms privileged couples, followed by children's rooms, eventually filtering down to servant and staff quarters.

A unique feature of these homes—and which appeared in Leila's writing—is the central role of the "hoash," an open-air courtyard that functions as a social, saloon-like space and, on very hot nights, as an outdoor bedroom. *Lyrics Alley,* set during the waning days of the Anglo-Egyptian condominium, draws from her family history. Readers have a vivid glimpse of life in the saraya, which mimics Egyptian-style design and interiors, but also retains the typically Sudanese space of the hoash: "The wide, open-air hoash was lined with bed, little stools and tables. It was a massive kitchen, sitting room and bedroom in which women, servants and children cooked, slept and socialized."[11] Many pivotal moments of *Lyrics Alley* happen in or around the hoash. Interestingly, the book does not shy away from exposing a pervasive Egyptian cultural supremacy that was the norm despite generations of intermarriage, and a deeply felt sense of Sudanese identity.

Fuad Aboulela

By the time Mustafa's saraya was built and functioning, Fuad Mustafa Aboulela, the tenth and the youngest of his children, was already 27 years old. Born in November 1928, Fuad's childhood was spent in one of the beautiful traditional homes nestled in the Omdurman alleys. Despite the loss of his mother at the age of two, which was perhaps barely a memory, Fuad had a comfortable childhood. After his death in 2008, Leila would write in an homage that he "grew up in a teeming household, ten brothers and sisters, countless cousins, innumerable friends…sleeping in the open air, eating with his fingers, playing football in the alley."[12]

This convivial atmosphere notwithstanding, Fuad's life trajectory had been ordained right from the schools he would attend, to the career he would undertake, and the person he would marry. Mustafa may have been physically absent, but he was not a negligent parent, and the family's traditional structure meant that his wishes were obeyed and respected by his many children. Most older siblings tended to play a parental role due to significant age gaps, but Fuad was close in age to his sister Fawzia, and they were often treated as twins. They were also the generation that was spoiled by the success of the family business. Family members claim that they were the only kids to be dropped off at school in a car, at a time when hardly anyone in Khartoum owned one.

Fuad's high school years were spent in the footsteps of his older brothers at the posh, all-male, British boarding school Victoria College in Egypt's Alexandria. Founded in 1901, it started as a school exclusively for wealthy sons of businessmen, but with the introduction of Oxford and Cambridge qualifying exams, it soon became a pipeline for university education in England, Scotland and the US. The school's alumni include King Hussein ibn Talal of Jordan; Faisal II ibn Ghazi—the last Hashemite king of Iraq—and his uncle, the regent Abd al-Ilah; the former Sultan of Zanzibar; and the king of Albania.[13] Decades later, alumni and Palestinian intellectual Edward Said would describe it "as a school designed to be the Eton of the Middle East" where "[e]xcept for the teachers of Arabic and French, the faculty was entirely English," even though there were no English students enrolled.[14]

In *Lyrics Alley,* protagonist Nur attends Victoria College in the early fifties, and his father Mahmoud does not mind the exorbitant price of the elite school. "Every penny spent on the fees was worth this joy," he thinks. Mahmoud takes pride in the knowledge that his son excels at the British school and is considered an "all-rounder" by the headmaster. The patriarch enjoys seeing his son in a "navy school blazer with the letter V and C embroidered in gold on the pocket, the C underneath the letter V." Mahmoud's visits to Alexandria involve treating Nur and his friends to kebabs and koftas since the students were "not allowed such food in the dorms and they had to bribe the cleaning staff to buy them ful and falafel from outside. Poor boys, forced to eat English food every day: boiled potatoes, roast beef, and more tasteless boiled vegetables."[15]

Though the novel makes light of this type of cultural brainwashing, Fuad was not necessarily immune to these influences, and on visits back home, his family teased him about being too British and nicknamed him "John." But the Khartoum family were also proud of the fact that he attended Victoria College, and he was often accosted by the elderly who asked him about world events since he could read English-language newspapers.

In *Lyrics Alley,* Nur's illustrious life trajectory is interrupted by a tragic swimming accident, and Mahmoud leverages Victoria College's powerful networks to make sure that his son is admitted to the Egyptian hospital where "students were entitled to the same amenities as the British staff and Army personnel."[16]

Nonetheless, the other Aboulela men successfully completed their schooling at Victoria College and went on to pursue university. But his older brother Saad was unable to attend Oxford, despite securing admission, because of the outbreak of World War II. Since Fuad was much younger, his studies were not interrupted by these global events, and he completed his university degree at Trinity College in Dublin. Fuad remembers the Dublin years as cold, alienating and riddled with discomfort—uncannily similar to how his daughter Leila would experience London and Aberdeen, almost 50 years later. Gone was the warmth of North Africa, or the luxury of Victoria College, and of the Omdurman home. But he obtained a master's in economics nonetheless, and respite came in the form of a return to Khartoum in the mid-fifties, just as Sudan gained independence from Britain and Egypt on January 1, 1956.

Fuad joined his brothers in developing and modernizing the Aboulela businesses, slowly and steadily moving them away from agriculture. It was during this time that the massive Aboulela office complex sprang up on Jamhurriya Street in downtown Khartoum, and the family secured a coveted Mercedes-Benz franchise, making them the only dealers of Mercedes in Sudan. Though the arrival of the deluxe German cars was welcomed by wealthy families, it was the trucks supplied by the company that were the game-changers. Not only were Mercedes-Benz trucks beneficial for their ongoing trade in cotton and gum arabic, but they also became a staple in the country. In Khartoum, a Mercedes fixation can be observed to this day, with a street named after the company and a Mercedes-Benz Club of car lovers with almost 7000 active members.[17]

On his personal life, his wife Mona paints Fuad as a man who knew his own mind, especially about marriage. Arranged marriage did not appeal to Fuad, but Mustafa was keen to line up suitable women from the upper echelons of society for his son. Once, Mustafa hosted a small gathering at home with the daughter of the head of a major Egyptian bank in Khartoum. Fuad did not refuse to join in, but when the guests were about to arrive, he escaped out the window and drove off, leaving an irate Mustafa to spend time with the guests by himself. Fuad dreamed of an Egyptian wife familiar with Sudan, a hybrid of both cultures much like him. Unwittingly, he found her when his sister introduced him to Mona Khalifa. She had lived in Sudan for several years with her parents as a teenager and was bewitched by the Sudanese countryside. She fantasized about marrying a Sudanese man who liked Egyptian women. Independent of his father, Fuad had found his match.

Mona Khalifa

Mona was born on March 21, 1943, in Cairo to Abdelfattah Khalifa and Leila Moharram. Theirs was a middle-class home where education and academic achievement were valued above all else. Mona's mother had secured admission to medical school and had started attending university. However, once she married, she had been forbidden from continuing her education by her in-laws. Abdelfattah and Leila were thus determined that they would never let their bright daughter's intellectual journey be disrupted by such traditions.

Still, the Moharram side of the family remained a point of pride for Mona. She respected her quiet and determined maternal grandmother, who was dedicated to her household of three daughters and one son, and for Mona, she was also a picture of quintessential Egyptian poise, languidly sipping coffee on her balcony.

Mona never met her maternal grandfather, but she had seen photos of him and knew that Ali Moharram was an engineer who worked in the railways and was fascinated by the information that he liked translating the works of Charles Dickens from English to Arabic. Not only was this side of the family connected to the English language—something that would play a large role in Mona's life when she pursued education in the UK—but the Moharram family spent several years in Atbara, in northern

Sudan, described as "the city of 'iron and fire' at the heart of Sudan's railway network."[18] Ali worked here for many years, and all his children were born there as well, thus establishing a family history in Sudan, and a connection that Mona only learned about many years later when she adopted Sudan as her home.

Abdelfattah's father, Khalifa, hailed from a small village. But after completing his studies at Al-Azhar University, he moved to Cairo to work as an Arabic and religion teacher. His wife Hosna bore him six children; out of these, the oldest son, Kamal, and the youngest son, Baha, were to test the family's patience and will to an extraordinary degree. Baha, an intelligent and vibrant person, progressively became paralyzed as a child—a condition attributed to problems during his birth that led to a lack of oxygen supply to his brain. While he was the cause of much melancholy and stress regarding caregiving, the older son Kamal's choices led to tragedy and heartbreak for the Khalifa patriarch.

Kamal was the first to get a degree in the US, but after he returned from Egypt, he joined the Muslim Brotherhood and scaled the ranks of the organization very quickly. Things fell apart rather speedily after he was implicated in the 1954 plot to assassinate Gamal Abdel Nasser, which was then "used as a pretext to crush the Muslim Brotherhood: a number of its members were executed and hundreds were imprisoned under brutal conditions."[19] Kamal was imprisoned without trial, and the government refused to tell the family where he was being held.

Mona was old enough to remember the shift in mood and tensions in the household mounting as her grandfather went from prison to prison across the country in hopes of finding his son. He became gaunt and miserable, and cast a dark shadow over the home. Abdelfattah, by then a professor of agriculture, often accompanied him on these travels. Eventually, they found Kamal in the Western Desert in inhumane condition, with clear indications that he had been severely tortured. Mona calls this a "turning point" in the ethos and value system of the Khalifa family. While her grandfather never really recovered from those years and remained heartbroken until his death in the seventies, her father, Abdelfattah, disavowed religion, became quick to observe signs of fanaticism in people, and even stopped going to the mosque.

The years leading up to this family tragedy, however, were productive, even exciting, since her father, Abdelfattah, got an opportunity to pursue his PhD in Cambridge, in the UK. Mona has blurry memories of these four years. It was a long journey by ship, and she vaguely remembers Britain in the late forties as bleak, with long lines for provisions as the country attempted to rebuild after World War II.

Upon return to Egypt, Abdelfattah first worked in a rural part but then got a faculty position at the plush campus of Ain Shams University, located in one of the palace grounds of King Farouk. Even though the school was Mona's happy place, and she has fond memories of playing violin and having lots of friends, the Nasser assassination plot continued to haunt the Khalifa family as the government continued a crackdown on what was deemed as "terrorist activities." This involved spying on university staff. Given Abdelfattah's close connection to these events, he accepted a position at the University of Khartoum's Shambat campus and relocated his family to Sudan in 1957. Mona was 14 years old and her younger brothers, Moharram and Mahmud, were seven and three.

Air travel between Cairo and Khartoum had only recently begun, and what now takes a little over two hours amounted to a seven-hour journey. Naturally, Mona and her younger brothers were excited to be on a plane for the first time. In contrast to her life growing up in a Cairo apartment, Mona's memory of her teen years in Sudan is idyllic, filled with serene and picturesque landscapes. She would often ride her bike alongside the Nile and vividly remembers a rainy, beautiful day by the river, where—having fallen in love with the land and the softness of its rhythms—she conjured the fantasy of a Sudanese husband. "I really wanted to stay," Mona confesses.

It would only be five more years before she would tie the knot with Fuad, who was 16 years older but a dashing and wealthy Sudanese bachelor. The Aboulela family came in from Khartoum for the lavish wedding held at the new Hilton Hotel in Cairo in 1962. They made a chic couple, with a slim, coiffed Mona sporting the tightly fitted midi dresses fashionable at the time, and Fuad in button-down shirts and slacks, with stylish Sirmont frame glasses.

They chose to become a nuclear family unit and moved to the well-heeled Al-Amarat neighborhood in Khartoum, a leafy and plush area with wide avenues, lined with the homes of diplomats from the neighboring embassies. But the extended family was only a short car ride away, and weekend dinners, special occasions, and celebrations in the Omdurman saraya remained an integral part of the couple's lives.

Mona's preoccupation with her studies immediately set her apart from everyone else. After completing high school in Khartoum, Mona had been living with her aunt Soraya, her mother's sister, in Cairo and was almost ready to graduate with a degree in pharmacy when the marriage proposal came. A brilliant student and the apple of her father's eye, Mona was certainly ambitious and determined to succeed in her education. Though the modest and middle-class Khalifas were overjoyed to marry their daughter into the wealthy Aboulela family, Abdelfattah asserted that his daughter would not suffer the same fate as his wife. In fact, most of Mona's familial milestones—whether marriage, pregnancy—are punctuated with stories of an impending exam that she was either preparing for or sitting.

With the move back to Khartoum after her wedding, Mona's studies were interrupted, since the Cairo-operated university there did not offer a degree in pharmacy. Guided by her father, Mona switched to statistics, which would allow her to earn a doctorate in demography at the London School of Economics almost 14 years later. Statistics would also come to dominate her daughter Leila's life, since Mona would control all academic turns for her daughter, until Leila slowly but determinedly broke free, suddenly publishing a novel at the late age of thirty-five.

Notes

1 Leila Aboulela, *River Spirit* (Grove Atlantic: 2023), 274.
2 Robert O. Collins, *A History of Modern Sudan* (Cambridge University Press: 2008), 21–25.
3 The word used in Arabic was "fuhool" which translates to stallion.
4 Robert O. Collins, *A History of Modern Sudan* (Cambridge University Press: 2008), 29.
5 Harold D. Nelson, *Sudan: A Country Study*. (Washington, D.C.: U.S. Govt. Print. Off.: 1982), 178, https://catalog.hathitrust.org/Record/001544141
6 Interview (joint) with Awad Aboulela and Abda Basheer, in-person, Khartoum, July 2, 2022.
7 "The Sennar Dam and the Gezira Irrigation Project." *Nature,* vol. 117 (1926): 200–201, and "The Sennar Dam and the Gezira Irrigation Scheme." *The Engineer,* (1924).
8 Abdelmoneim, Yousra, "The Life and Legacy of Saad Mustafa Aboulela." https://substack.com/@yousraabdelmoneim/p-184265948
9 Unpublished personal essay by Zeinab Elbakri.
10 "Sudan's Booming Cement Industry," *Sudanow Magazine*, February 25, 2018, https://sudanow-magazine.net/page.php?Id=379
11 Leila Aboulela, *Lyrics Alley* (Phoenix/Orion Books: 2010), 16.
12 Leila Aboulela, "A Mention of My Father," *Jalada 09: Nostalgia*, December 4, 2020, https://jaladaafrica.org/2020/12/04/a-mention-of-my-father-by-leila-aboulela/
13 Alain Silvera, "Victoria College," in *Encyclopedia of the Modern Middle East and North Africa* (Macmillan Reference USA: 2004).
14 Edward Said, *Out of Place: A Memoir*, (Alfred Knopf: 1999), 16.
15 Leila Aboulela, *Lyrics Alley* (Phoenix/Orion Books: 2010), 42.
16 Leila Aboulela, *Lyrics Alley* (Phoenix/Orion Books: 2010), 100.
17 "Sudan's German Car Obsession," report by Adrian Kriesch, posted May 25, 2022, by DW REV—Cars & Mobility, YouTube, https://www.youtube.com/watch?v=2JfqS8i_uJc
18 Mohammed Amin, "Sudan's city of iron and fire comes to the capital on a train," *Middle East Eye*, April 24, 2019, https://www.middleeasteye.net/news/sudans-city-iron-and-fire-comes-capital-train
19 Phil Gurski, "October 26, 1954: Attempted assassination of Egyptian President Nasser," *Borealis Threat & Risk Consulting*, October 26, 2021, https://borealisthreatandrisk.com/october-26-1954-attempted-assassination-of-egyptian-president-nasser/

2 Mothers and Daughters

A Khartoum Girlhood

"The good thing about Leila is that she is not a rebel."

Mona Khalifa observed her 13-year-old daughter, recalling Leila's visit to London during the three years that Mona lived there as a PhD student. Leila was obedient and easy to care for, unlike her more boisterous younger brother, and the mother and daughter spent over a month in the tiny hostel room, taking turns sleeping on the bed and getting used to the shared bathroom. Hanging around bored was not Mona's idea of how Leila should spend her summer, and an optimal use of her daughter's time was a priority for her. So she enrolled Leila in an advanced English writing class—and while teen girls may not have been officially allowed to attend, Leila had always been unusually tall and sometimes passed as older than her actual age in those days.

Despite an English-medium education in Khartoum, Mona wanted her daughter to read "proper books," and advance formally in both subjects. Mother and daughter took the bus to the writing class on the first day. But after that, Leila was on her own. Each morning, she put a ten-pence coin into the slot and went across town to a class populated primarily by senior citizens. She was clearly the youngest, and the teacher did not allow her to go out into the city for her lunch break, so she brought a packed lunch and ate at a designated place.

Evenings were meant to be fun, but Leila did not have friends in London, and the only television set was in the common social area. Mona did not want her teen daughter spending time there because the other women residents brought their boyfriends over and indulged in risqué activities. She rented a small television set, and evenings found the quiet and unobtrusive Leila in front of the screen with American TV series like *Happy Days* or *Hawaii Five-O* for company, and on some days, the far more exciting *Top of the Pops.* Leila found herself addicted to Jean Plaidy novels and remembers buying entire sets of the British historical romances.

DOI: 10.4324/9781003306719-3

Figure 2.1 Leila and Mona, London, 1977

The summer in London was one of many such sojourns that mother and daughter would embark on over the years. For the pensive teenager, Mona's well-intentioned authority over all the big and small aspects of her life was normal and understood as the love of an educated and ambitious mother, razor-focused on a solid academic path for her daughter. Theirs was a bond in the double sense of the word; certainly, there was a connection and trust, but there was also the strain that emerged from Mona's controlling habits, as Leila became an adult herself.

It is unsurprising, then, that stories of mothers and daughters are often at the core of Leila's fiction. The strong mother and sometimes a less willful daughter are recurring tropes in the short stories about the mother-daughter duo Nadia and Lateefa. The two generations of mothers in *Minaret* stage Lamya and her mother Doctora Zeinab as mirror opposites of the timid and self-doubting protagonist Najwa. Perhaps these apprehensive women protagonists stem from "having a strong, powerful mother who was always outshining me," Leila said. Among kind yet overbearing mothers, the mother-in-law Mahasen, in *The Translator,* as well as the two mothers, Waheeba and Nabilah, in *Lyrics Alley,* also expose Leila's ambivalent, complex, yet nonetheless deep attachment to the mother figure.

***

Mona, marriage, and motherhood

Post-independence Sudan was changing. The sixties and seventies were marked by turmoil, and the start of coups and countercoups that have since become an unfortunate feature of Sudanese politics. Despite the economic and financial instability, the Gezira irrigation scheme ensured that the agricultural arm of the Aboulela family business continued to grow. Around the same time, the massive Aboulela Commercial Building in the downtown business district in Khartoum's Gamhurriya Street was completed in 1956.[1] Designed by Greek architect George Stefanides, it was a formidable symbol of the wealth and power of the Aboulela family.[2] The office complex was also indicative of the architecture boom at the time. It joined several small and large construction projects spurred by the establishment of the Department of Architecture at the University of Khartoum and the sincere—though uneven—efforts of the government to develop and modernize the country.

The Aboulela family was growing, and with the births of children and grandchildren, the gorgeous and bustling Omdurman saraya was now in full use. Like some of the others from the younger generation of the large and expanding Aboulela family, Mona and Fuad chose to become a nuclear unit, and make their home in the affluent residential neighborhood of Al-Amarat in Khartoum. City life was designed to be more European and suited the couple's cosmopolitan sense of themselves. Fuad, now in his late thirties, had found an ideal partner in young Mona, whose Cairo sensibility, along with a love of Sudan, matched his dual desire to enjoy the lifestyle of Sudan's former colonizers, Egypt and England, while staying rooted in Sudanese culture.

Married life in Khartoum was comfortable and freeing for Mona. Much like her father, her husband encouraged Mona's academic ambitions—a unique privilege that she did not take for granted, given the patriarchal, traditional, and bourgeois family she had married into, as well as the acute and near-constant awareness of how her own mother had been forced to quit medical school after marriage.

Mona's commitment to her own education was staunch. By the time the offer of marriage came from the Aboulela family, Mona had already completed almost two years of her degree in Pharmacy at a university in Cairo. Mona's father had made his son-in-law promise that his daughter would continue studying, and perhaps even work after marriage. Fuad did not resist. In fact, he proved just how committed he was to Mona's education in March 1964, on the day his father, Mustafa Aboulela, passed away. An eight-month-pregnant Mona was certain she would miss her university exams as the funeral procession blocked several Omdurman streets, and mourners thronged the family saraya. A clever Fuad, skilled at escaping his father's best-laid traps when he was alive, arranged for a cousin to sneak his wife from out the back of the home to be driven to the university.

Even after the end of the Anglo-Egyptian condominium, the universities in Khartoum remained under the administrative and curricular control of Egyptian and English universities for several years, with patronage and funding to professors who worked in both places during the academic year. Mona's pharmacy course at Cairo University was unavailable in the same university's Khartoum branch. After her wedding and move back to Sudan, Mona started her university studies from scratch in Khartoum, this time enrolling in the Statistics major, which would slowly but systematically coalesce into a PhD in Demography almost two decades later.

Fuad seemed to like having a wife who was so intellectually oriented, and relished being married to a woman who would end up with a very high education and career success. Despite being half his age and from a significantly less wealthy background, her superior standing as an Egyptian in Sudan and her unique drive for academic success made this a marriage between equals. If taking exams, earning degrees, and embarking on a scholarly career was a love language, Fuad and Mona were fluent in it.

Only a year had passed since Mona's wedding to Fuad. Pregnancy suited Mona Khalifa, and the months preceding the birth of her firstborn, Leila, felt natural and relaxed. Soon after her university exams, she traveled back to her parents' place in Cairo, since it was customary for the daughter to be near her mother for the birth of her first child. A healthy baby girl arrived at dawn on May 2, 1964, greeted by Mona's mother, who had spent the night with her laboring daughter. Newborn Leila was named after her grandmother and spent the traditional first 40 days with her mother and grandparents in Cairo. Fuad flew in from Khartoum almost right away, filled with pride and joy for his wife and newborn daughter.

Leila was born into a duality; the soft and unhurried rhythm of Sudanese life all around her alongside the rigor of ambitious parents given her mother's academic endeavors and her father's expanding business. That only two months before her birth, her parents conspired to ensure that her mother would be able to sit for her exams as the Aboulela patriarch's

Figure 2.2 Baby Leila and Mona

funeral took place was indicative of the two spaces in which Leila's childhood unfolded.

Mona kept herself on task and set about looking for a nanny who would travel back to Khartoum with them. The large and efficient Husna appeared like a blessing in Mona's life, and they traveled to Khartoum, where a sparkling new bungalow awaited the trio in Al-Amarat. Fuad had purchased the villa, and Mona was happily surprised. This is where the growing family would spend two decades.

Like many of the homes in the neighborhood, the bungalow was modeled in the popular architectural style of tropical modernism, which blended the simplicity and minimalism of modernism with design details that accommodated the tropical environment. Developed in the sixties, Al-Amarat was a symbol of modern and prosperous city life, as the two-story bungalows and manicured gardens were completely different from the more rudimentary, one-level structures of the traditional Sudanese homes in which Fuad had spent his childhood in Omdurman. The spacious and cool Aboulela bungalow was flanked by tiled verandas and iron gates that would swing open and shut several times a day for the family car. Immediately neighboring the Aboulelas on the quiet tree-lined street was the Jordanian embassy, with the ambassador's residence right next to it. Across from them was a large square of land that remained empty and open until it was developed in the 2000s.

Husna lived up to her impressive credentials. She had worked for an Egyptian ambassador in Moscow and was disciplined and experienced. She placed the mother and baby daughter on a strict schedule of nursing and naps, much to Mona's delight. Leila was characterized as a calm and happy baby who was never fussy or unnecessarily demanding. Black-and-white photos of a bright-eyed Husna holding Leila and of a glowing mother, Mona, sporting a short bob in chic sleeveless dresses are lovingly assembled in Leila's well-preserved family albums today.

Even though Husna set Mona on the track for the exact kind of motherhood that suited her personality and scholarly ambitions, her stay only lasted a couple of years, and she left before Khalid was born. She longed to be with her own children back in Egypt and expressed a whiff of nostalgia for Moscow's cooler climes rather than Sudan's intense heat. By then, Mona had resumed her studies, and the nuclear family had settled into the new house, establishing a daily routine that continued with the birth of Khalid in 1966, two years later, and carried on with both kids in school.

The school years

Leila's education began in earnest, with Mona unilaterally in charge. From a young age, there would be no deviation from the paths, institutions, subjects, and entrance exams chosen for Leila right up until a 30-something-year-old Leila finally broke loose by underperforming in academia and slowly but perhaps willfully turning away from becoming the person her mother desired her to be. As would be typical for a bourgeois family in almost any postcolonial country, Leila's education was a combination of various colonial systems starting with St. Francis, a fairly regular Sudanese elementary school with Arabic instruction, run by

European nuns and priests; followed by The American School that was run by and populated with Americans; and finally, the Sisters School, an all-girls, Catholic school run, once again, by strict European nuns.

At home and in the broader social world, there was an instilling of Egyptian cultural superiority—a mindset that had barely changed since Egypt's occupation and domination over Sudan from the 1820s to 1956. Whether it was the fashionable frocks brought from Cairo for little Leila, the daily meals at home, the regular holidays in various parts of Egypt, or Mona's ties to the universities there, there was an ever-present notion that everything Egyptian was simply better. Mona pushed a ubiquitous Egyptian-ness on her children, who were fluent in all Egyptian ways.

Maybe it was not fun spending time in an apartment in Cairo—as opposed to the luxurious villa in Khartoum—or maybe it was Mona's nervous intensity around all of it, but young Leila associated Egypt with an oppressive sort of "fixity," a space in which she could easily do something that her mother would disapprove of. In contrast, she began equating her father with something quintessentially Sudanese—a softness and freedom that she would come to yearn for over time, and that became vaguely inscribed in her as an authentic Sudan. Several years later, she would express these two troubled and slippery nodes of her identity through the difficult dynamic between two mothers in her third novel, *Lyrics Alley:* the educated, posh, and brittle Nabilah and the traditional, tough, and less refined Waheeba.

The early memories of Leila's first school, St. Francis, are particularly happy, despite the typical severe, disciplinary atmosphere of the school. In contrast, the American School was a source of stress and anxiety for Leila, while her younger brother Khalid was miserable and came home crying every single day from St. Francis, leaving Mona scrambling for solutions to fix the problem.

Mona, who had received her degree in Statistics by then, suddenly found herself in an unusual phase of academic inactivity. With a lot more socializing on her calendar, she had found the American School through her friend, also named Mona. Usually reserved for children of the US embassy staff, the school had decided to open to Sudanese students. She enrolled both kids in the American School, as did her friend. The two Monas secured part-time teaching jobs at the school, with Mona teaching Mathematics and her friend teaching Physical Education.

The American School was a veritable lap of luxury, a far cry from the normalcy and the modest ambiance of Leila's previous school. In its early days, the school was housed in a villa in Al-Amarat before becoming a purpose-built compound many years later. Despite being shiny, air-conditioned, and incredibly well-resourced, Leila had a bumpy start. She was held back one grade since the school determined that her English

Figure 2.3 Leila, Mona, and Fuad

was not at the required level. This put her mother in overdrive; Leila was made to do extra prep so she could catch up with students her age, and Mona advocated on her behalf until Leila was finally placed in the correct grade. But Leila's difficulties were really on the social level, starting with her having left easygoing Sudanese students just like her, only to stick out like a sore thumb in an American school made up of mostly the children of embassy staff.

A seven-year-old Leila had never felt more like an outsider at a school she described as a "strange bubble" of Americanness. Leila stood out in

Figure 2.4 Leila, age 9, at The American School, Khartoum

her dresses and sandals, while the other kids wore shorts and sneakers, and despite her parents' good English, her schoolmates' references and communication style were completely new to the little girl. The Americans strode through the school with a complete sense of ownership, and their exotic lunches, wrapped in aluminum foil and with ingredients often flown in from the US, were fascinating for little Leila. The four years spent at this school remain seared in Leila's mind. She remembers American teachers telling her furious mother that Leila was "retarded" since she did not say very much and was not caught up in math class. She also recalls a blond boy nicknaming her "Disease," a cruel and racist slur that stuck for a while.

Leila did not have a name for the way she was perceived and treated, but it was at the snobby and white American school that she first encountered racism. In fact, after the publication of her second novel, *Minaret*, in 2005, and the US' Islamophobic War on Terror in full swing, Leila would write her harshest pronouncement upon the school and upon the US in an essay titled "America, Owner of the Moon" (2004) that never found a publisher. In it, she recounts the racism, the anti-Blackness, and the utter arrogance of a school that barely knew it was located in Sudan and on the African continent. "The school was for American children, it gave them an American education," she wrote. "Inside the school, you could forget you were in poverty-stricken Africa and glide through air-conditioned American culture. What was I doing there?" It seemed that these strange feelings of humiliation and anger had resurfaced almost 15 years later when she became marked as a Muslim and migrant after leaving Sudan and moving to the UK for her husband Nadir's job.

When asked how she perceived herself during these childhood years, Leila admits that she was a fundamentally shy person and adds that "my perception is that I'm holding back." Always plagued by a sense that it was safer not to speak up, speak out, or fight for her way, the act of "holding back" remains a singularly clear feeling that she associates with that time. What Leila calls a "cosseted lifestyle" that did not require her to be independent or venture out into the public certainly compounded her timid sense of self, which eventually found expression in many of the women characters in her fiction.

But there were good bits too; places, habits, and relationships that would endure over the years. The first among the positive aspects was a library filled with English-language books, and the second was a compassionate teacher named Floyce Abdelwahab, an African American woman married to a Sudanese man. The cumulative effect of the two was that reading officially entered Leila's life as an activity that would absorb her and allow her to get away from the anxieties she was experiencing in the alien environment.

The other positive aspect was the young teacher Floyce, who was herself an object of discrimination in the elite school, turned Leila onto a different America, one that articulated the Black experience and honest truths about racism. Mona was also fond of her and found her to be a good influence on her daughter, drawing Leila out of her shell. Leila admits that Floyce may have been the first person to instill in her a sort of "political awareness" by speaking about the history of race and slavery in the US with stories of Malcolm X, even taking Leila to the American Center for a screening of the film *Roots*. Leila admits, "I read a lot of books, I found out that I loved reading and maybe that made me the writer I am today. I learned about Thanksgiving, Anne Frank, slavery, the Boston Tea Party, something about George Washington and a tree."[3] Furthermore, since the beloved teacher always insisted on being called Mrs. Abdelwahab, and eagerly embraced her Sudanese, and thus her African identity, it allowed for Leila's bruised pride about being Sudanese to be healed, after having been shamed and othered by her classmates.

Floyce and the world she inhabited made a strong impression on Leila, and a vaguely Floyce-like figure and a certain kind of American microcosm in Khartoum appeared in one of her short stories called "Baby Love," published in *Wasafiri* magazine.[4] In the story, young Majda is in love with Sameer, who is studying abroad. She meets Sameer's African American mother, Janet, for lunch. Pleased, yet insecure about this meeting, Majda's afternoon at Khartoum's American Club is spent being talked down to by Janet, who finds her son far too young and far too much of a catch for Majda. Many of the core themes in Leila's fiction appear here—an unsure female protagonist, overly aware of her mediocrity and not comfortable in her own skin; a dominating mother figure who is the mirror opposite of the protagonist, and is thus confident, intimidating, smug, and overly sure of herself; and also the underlayer of social satire, as the narrator's keen eye catches people and places at their most unguarded moments.

Janet, of course, is nothing like Floyce, except that she is married to a Sudanese man. Janet carries herself with the same sense of entitlement that Leila observed at her school and came to view as something very American. Americans also give mixed messages. For example, Janet asks to be called by her first name as a mark of her casual nature, yet there is nothing casual or easy within an interaction steeped in hierarchies and perceived class differences. But the decor of Janet's home and the cultural references were all derived from Leila's memories of Floyce.

> Everything in the house was from America; the furniture and the videotapes. Even the drink Sameer gave me, he said it was called Kool-Aid. His room had a poster of Malcolm X who I didn't know and Bob Marley who I did...In the sitting room we watched an early Soul Train on which The Supremes sang "Baby Love" while Janet flicked through the pages of Ebony. I loved that magazine when I looked at it. "You can take it, I'm all done with it," Janet said. I took Ebony with me to school and showed it off to my friends. We had never seen a magazine like that before. Girls who looked like us but were so glamorous, so obviously Western.[5]

When Floyce passed away in 2016, Leila wrote a short dedication on Facebook recounting how much she admired her "tastefully decorated home." As in the story, she also wrote that Floyce lent her copies of *Ebony* magazine and introduced her to a cool American television show called *Soul Train*—an exemplar of a subculture that might have instilled in her a Black and Afro pride, sprinkled with a large helping of glamor.[6] It would have also woken Leila up to an exciting world beyond the one of British and Egyptian influences that was part of her daily life, and likely taken for granted.

There are two other aspects of "Baby Love" that reveal the spaces and preoccupations of Leila's Khartoum girlhood. First, the American Club, a setting that also shows up in her novel *Minaret*, was where Leila did a lot of socializing and growing up, even eventually falling in love with Nadir Mahjoub. Yet another variation of the sort of elite, expensive, and colonial country clubs that still abound in previously colonized countries, the American Club was an idyllic and cheerful setting with a glorious pool, burgers and sundaes on the menu, themed parties, weekly movie nights, and a curious coterie of international, expat-types buzzing about.

In *Minaret*, the twins, Najwa and Omar, are shown to be the archetypal rich Khartoum brats, and there are references to them partying into the wee hours at the American Club disco or reminiscing about costume parties. The Aboulelas gained membership through their connections with the American school, as well as their significant wealth and standing in the upper echelons of Sudanese society. It became their daily favorite, with evenings spent with friends as kids swam in the pool or watched the latest American movies.

Second, "Baby Love," like several of the other early stories, also captures Leila's long-standing preoccupation with domineering and complex mother figures. Even her teacher, Floyce, and the world she inhabited as an African American in Sudan become an opportunity to generate an irritable and condescending mother figure, through Janet.

While Leila was at the American School and enjoying the American Club, her usually ambitious and focused mother Mona was going through a phase that was so bizarre to those around her—and so unlike her usual self—that Leila remembers it vividly, despite being so young. It took a stern intervention to make Mona change course.

Mona had completed her master's degree and appeared to be at loose ends with regard to her career, despite her part-time teaching role at the American School. With her and her kids ensconced there, the upscale social milieu of the American Club became part and parcel of their daily life. For a few short years, Mona tried out a "good wife and socialite" routine, even though the shoe did not quite fit. Giggling about this strange time in her life at the age of eighty, Mona recounts that she had always felt envious of the seemingly relaxed lifestyles of wealthy Khartoum wives, who spent their days making themselves look good for their husbands, and coming up with novelties to test out in their modern kitchens. A "life of leisure," as she called it, comprised a nonstop whirl of coffee parties, regular parties, hanging out at the club, and cookery meetups. The town had many expats during those days, and socializing happened at the various country clubs for Syrians, Egyptians, British, and so on. Mona decided to learn how to make cakes for her kids—but, more importantly, to impress the other wives at Monday afternoon's group cookouts.

Unsurprisingly, her innately ambitious nature got the better of her, and she began to go overboard. During a visit to Egypt, she found a reputed bakery in Cairo and employed their chef to give her lessons every week at her parents' home. Week after week, the chef would come armed with all the baking ingredients, and together, he and Mona would whip up fabulous cakes.

But Abdelfattah Khalifa, her father, lost his patience and sat his daughter down. He explained that he had not worked hard to ensure his daughter was well-educated only to be regaled with cakes. He also reminded her that he had made a promise to her husband Fuad that his daughter would be able to study and pursue a career. And then, he delivered the fatal blow: he told Mona that she had disappointed him. Shaken by her father's admonishment and shocked out of her humdrum social rhythm and competitive housewife spirit, Mona soon eased herself out of this pleasant, but intellectually somnolent lifestyle. She now set her sights on a PhD.

Adolescent angst

The unhappy years at the American School slowly faded from memory once Leila joined the bustling, cheerful, and social environment of the Sisters' School in the seventh grade. The girls-only Roman Catholic Mission school was located in a vibrant part of Khartoum, close to the university and the Republican Palace, right across from the Nile. Catholic missions were established in Sudan in the early 1900s. Founded in 1928, the school was run and staffed by white, European nuns, and they provided English-language education, grounded in Catholic values, to a Muslim-majority student body.

The explicit goal of colonial administrators was to provide the upper and upper middle-class sections of the colonized society with a mandated European education, so that this elite, educated class would be put to the service of the colonial administration. Even today, religious, Christian education in the colonial language is available and popular across almost every country previously colonized by Europeans. The image of these school systems as bastions of elitism has also persisted into the 21st century; to date, it is practically common-sense knowledge among the upwardly mobile that these Catholic schools provide the best and most prestigious education one's child can receive.

Leila was now almost 12 years old and towered over her classmates. Her height was surprising since neither parent was particularly tall. Within the Aboulela home and within Leila's life, there was a return to normalcy, a restoration of the status quo. Mona had been jolted out of her socialite-housewife phase and had now decided to pursue a PhD at the London School of Economics. Fuad, of course, encouraged Mona's plans, and they set about making various tweaks and adjustments to the home

Figure 2.5 Leila, age 12, Sisters School, Khartoum

system. Arrangements with the domestic staff ensured a smooth school routine, but it soon became an extended family affair. Mona's father was so overjoyed by his daughter's admission into the PhD program that he rose to the challenge of taking care of her younger brothers in Cairo so that her mother could care for the grandchildren in Khartoum. Trips to London were also planned.

For Mona, this was a return to a country she had spent time in as a child, whose values and academic rigor she respected and aspired to. Serendipitously, her father was invited to London for a workshop at that time. He used the visit to set up a bank account for Mona, in the hopes of easing her move: all she had to do was sign and activate the account to access the deposit he left for her. But despite the planned smoothness, the day was not without its hiccups. After Mona dragged her suitcase up to the third floor of the tiny hostel room, she heard some kids playing at the school next door. Suddenly, it dawned on her that she had left her kids behind, and she was completely alone. She called Fuad and announced that she would like to come back, through desperate tears. Fuad reassured her she would be fine; he also reminded her of the material and emotional investments that had been made to realize her dream, that this was their "project" as a family, one that she couldn't thwart. It took some time, but she lost her self-consciousness around the shifts being made to accommodate her ambitions. Eventually she became self-assured and determined and told herself she deserved everything.

Mona dedicated herself to a strict study routine. She was not particularly social, and the international students from places like Ethiopia, Iran, or Egypt were primarily male. She recalls that she could not focus on making friends because she felt a sense of time ticking, given how much systemic overhaul had occurred to facilitate her obtaining this doctorate degree from a prestigious British university. The extraordinary levels of dedication and effort it took from the entire family for this young mother of two to pursue her dreams were not lost on Mona.

In Sudan, Leila was entering a comfortable teen girlhood with a group of friends at the Sisters' School, and a thriving social life at the American Club. Polaroid photos of a gaggle of schoolgirls with their arms around each other capture a radiantly happy Leila. All the girls are in a uniform of white, short-sleeved shirts over navy, knee-length pinafores belted at the waist; the crisp ironing appears to have come undone at the end of the school day. Leila sports a short bob of soft curls and is the only one in the group wearing glasses, which gives her an innocent, scholarly look compared to the more flirtatious glances of her friends as they pose for the camera. Even in the official annual school photos with the nuns, Leila is the epitome of cheer, flashing a wide smile. The class photos themselves capture a quintessentially seventies, upper-class Sudan as neatly dressed young women, some with gold watches and gold earrings, and a variety of skin colors attest to a confluence of races and heritages in the country. A middle-parted, layered shoulder-length hairstyle clearly seems to be trending and appears to mimic European or American popular culture.

The world of Leila's girlhood is repeatedly evoked in her early stories and novels, and she has admitted her attachment:

> I like writing about Khartoum and the Khartoum I grew up in. It's because my memories of it are very vivid. And I want to tell other people about it. The world doesn't know much about Khartoum. It's not a city people know about, it doesn't have a particularly good image, perhaps. That makes me even more keen to describe it, to describe the kind of beauty I felt I experienced when I was living there.[7]

A rose-tinted nostalgia may be very much at play here, but the clarity of her memories, and her desire to hold on to their beauty illustrates that these few years in Leila's life were particularly freeing, joyful, and unhindered by emotional and material burdens. So, it is not teenage woes or coming-of-age narratives that play a particularly big part in Leila's fiction; it is more the depiction of a vibrant Khartoum milieu that interests her.

Insofar as Leila explores teenage life, three challenging aspects of her adolescence tend to show up: having to start wearing glasses, developing a self-consciousness around being too tall, and, most importantly, the pressure to be slim. Young Soraya in *Lyrics Alley* and Farida in the short story "Farida's Eyes," both struggle with their vision, and finally get a prescription for glasses despite resistance from their not-so-well-off fathers. While Soraya feels womanlier, and even scholarly after acquiring her glasses, Farida confronts several adolescent issues at once. A diminutive and obedient student, Farida is forced to sit amongst the group of slacker back-benchers, because she is tall and thus should "not block the blackboard."[8]

Dieting and weight loss appear sporadically in some of the stories in the *Coloured Lights* collection. In the "The Boy from the Kebab Shop," the theme of dieting is directly sewn into the fabric of the mother-daughter relationship. Seventeen-year-old Dina has an attraction and repulsion to food:

> Her mother, Shushu, rarely cooked proper meals because she was always on a diet. Shushu imposed these diets on her daughter too who was even more overweight. The dieting made Dina continuously peckish, uneasy. She often binged on crisps and Mars bars, and the diets inevitably failed but they were never officially abandoned. Dieting had become a way of life, part of the house, part of the mother-daughter relationship.[9]

It is no surprise that Leila connects the teenage protagonist's uneasy and difficult relationship to food and dieting to that of her mother. Leila now makes light of these themes from her own childhood and laughingly recalls the pressure to be thin, attributing it directly to her own mother. Mona made it very clear that, since Leila was already too tall, she could not afford to be large. Additionally, Mona herself was trying out various fad diets during her phase as a Khartoum socialite and had herself lost a lot of weight. Leila remembers the "ridiculous" astronaut diet that was popular at the time, which involved devoting a day for just boiled eggs, another day for just fruits and so on. Over the course of many of her early works, Leila slowly chips away at the many angst-ridden preoccupations of her adolescence; mothers remain at the center of many of these experiences, with ambivalent daughters navigating a roulette of emotions that include respect, disdain, despair, resentment, envy, anger, but also love.

Among all of Leila's works, it is the novel *Minaret* that offers the most detailed perspectives on the lifestyles of the rich and young in Khartoum.

Najwa's upbringing comes closest to Leila's own privileged class background, and through her first-person perspective, the novel offers several snippets of life among Khartoum's wealthy youth as they hang out at the American Club, wear the latest fashion, smoke, drink, and dance into the late nights, swing in and out of large gated homes in their cars, and boast about various holidays abroad. But the fall from grace is swift and cruel, and life changes abruptly with her father's arrest and execution, her mother's demise, and her brother Omar's imprisonment for dealing drugs.

Even though she is always shown to be self-conscious and awkward, a now depressed Najwa finds herself putting on weight in London. Her despair worsens when she finds that her clothes no longer fit her as they used to; she is all alone, and bills are piling up. Najwa despondently finds herself reading a magazine called *Slimming*, pondering which diet would best suit her, and how many calories are in a spoon of ketchup. This preoccupation with dieting and looking good is meant to illustrate the wealthy, spoilt, young Najwa, while the mature and self-realized Najwa undergoes a transformation after she embraces Islam and slowly sheds the vanity of her youth, with the motif of dieting and weight loss functioning as a parable.

Mothers, mothering, and motherhood

Leila's mother remains an extraordinary force in her life, and many of her works appear dedicated to rendering the complex and multifaceted nature of mothers and motherhood. Two stories about the mother-daughter duo, Lateefa and Nadia, make their way into Leila's first published story collection titled *Colored Lights* in 2001. A third story about the same two characters was published in 2017 in the online magazine *Jalada,* and subsequently in her second story collection titled *Elsewhere, Home*, a year later.

In her novels, Mahasen, the mother-in-law, is a mother figure for Sammar in *The Translator*, and in *Minaret*, an orphaned Najwa is made the keen observer of the mother and daughter dynamics between Doctora Zeinab and Lamya. In *Lyrics Alley*, two mothers, the Sudanese Waheeba and the Egyptian Nabilah, compete for the attention of the husband that they share, and this becomes an opportunity to sketch out the cultural rivalries between the two countries as they play out within domestic, gendered spaces. Mothers are not an obvious focus in *The Kindness of Enemies* (2015) or in *The River Spirit* (2023), but the theme of motherhood does return with some intensity in Leila's work of speculative fiction *Bird Summons* (2019). In the novel, Moni has thrown away a thriving career, risking her marriage so she can be dedicated to caring for her son, Adam, who has severe cerebral palsy.

In Leila's fiction, mothers tend to be Egyptian, and thus deliberately project a cultural superiority that appears to become a site for the writer to work through her own conflicted Egyptian and Sudanese identity. Mona herself was staunchly Egyptian despite her love for her adopted country, Sudan. Leila recalls hearing the occasional heated argument between her parents and then fantasizing about a divorce that would force her to choose between her father (Sudan) and her mother (Egypt). The answer was always crystal clear to young Leila, who would declare her choice: Sudan.

The "fixity" of Egyptian culture, as she called it, and its perennial imposition is found in the overbearing Lateefa, who is raising her daughter Nadia in London. Lateefa and Nadia form a completely codependent family unit, where the father, Hamdy, barely figures. Any challenges within the relationship do not pose any threat to the core bond, nor do they engender any fantasies of rupture or escape.

The duo is first introduced in *Coloured Lights, in* the story "Tuesday Lunch." 8-year-old Nadia feels too timid to refuse the pork pie being served at school lunch and finds herself rather curious to taste the meat forbidden to Muslims. But soon Nadia is racked by so much guilt that she throws up in the classroom. Nadia is brought home by an unsuspecting Lateefa, who blames the incident on some old cream in the dessert. Mother and daughter share a moment of closeness over toast and tea in the middle of the night, as Nadia is left pondering her mother's extraordinary power: "Nadia thinks that her mother must have cast a spell on all the wrong things Nadia should not do. Bewitched pork pies, so that even when she wanted them, they, on their own accord, rejected her."[10]

The theme of being attracted to all things forbidden by her mother continues in the second story, "Make Your Own Way Home," where a grown-up Nadia visits her friend, Tracy, in a nursing home. Tracy has just had an abortion after getting pregnant out of wedlock, thus proving Lateefa's judgmental assessment of her to be true: "That girl Tracy is no good...She will have a bad end."[11] Her mother's directive that Nadia cut off from Tracy had only made Nadia more attracted to her. The nursing home becomes a way for Nadia to muse on her friendship with the liberal and easygoing English girl and to think through her own uneasy place as an Egyptian Muslim woman and migrant in England. Nadia's mind, desires, and movements are inadvertently influenced by her mother, who is stubbornly insistent that Nadia remain as Egyptian as possible in London. The sense of in-betweenness only deepens as the story progresses, with Nadia realizing she can neither connect with Tracy nor align with her mother.

A third iteration of the same duo appears several years later in the story "Summer Maze." The duo visits Cairo for the summer, and Nadia once again navigates her own in-betweenness as someone who is not fully

Egyptian nor quite English. This is, however, the first of the three stories where the reader enters Lateefa's perspective, and the author offers a sensitive portrait of a mother attempting to offer the best possible life for her daughter in a culturally different country. While Leila is conscious of the difficult and dominating nature of this mother, she renders her psychological complexities with empathy and softness. There is no doubt that the mother and daughter have an unshakeable bond despite the little irritations and eruptions.

Mother figures evolve rather differently in the novels that follow Leila's short story publications—though they retain many of the same traits—as do the daughters. In her first novel, *The Translator*, the protagonist Sammar refuses motherhood after the death of her husband: "She was unable to mother the child. The part of her that did the mothering had disappeared."[12] Crippled by her depression, Sammar places her son into the firm, capable, yet disapproving hands of her mother-in-law Mahsen. Sammar's abandonment of her son marks the epitome of her failure and inability to function without a husband, whereas Mahsen carries on despite the death of her son.

Mothers act. Daughters mull. Mothers are strong and steadfast, and daughters often have less agency and are not as self-assured.

In *The Translator*, Sammar eventually finds love, and thus her way back to her son and to her home. But the mother figure in this story is fixed: her identity and motivations do not change course even as catastrophic events unfold.

Mothers are just as fixed and unchanging in *Lyrics Alley,* but it is Leila's only novel where we get an explicitly binary representation of Egyptian versus Sudanese women. It is, inadvertently, also a portrait of the intensity of Egypt's colonial attitude toward Sudan and the Sudanese, which remains embedded within the Sudanese themselves. Mahmoud, the patriarch, is an ambitious businessman committed to expanding his fortunes in Sudan, which is on the cusp of independence from British and Egyptian control. His first wife, Waheeba, is a stereotype of a rural Sudanese woman with "tribal scars" on each cheek and "bangles of gold from her wrist to her elbow"[13] (LA, 16). She also was more "African in her features than her husband,"[14] a phrase meant to signal she was Black, rather than Mahmoud, who "was light-skinned enough to pass for an Egyptian."[15] Waheeba also prefers the traditional Sudanese lifestyle of the "hoash," the open-air space that includes the kitchen, living and sleeping areas.

Nabilah is Mahmoud's second wife and represents the antithesis of Waheeba. "An Egyptian city lady," Nabila was stylish in her European clothes, cosmopolitan, and educated.[16] She had rejected the life of the hoash, and had redesigned her wing in the Egyptian style, "not a Sudanese one." Condescending and snobbish, for her "Sudan was like the bottom of the sea, an exotic wilderness, soporific and away from the momentum of history. It was amazing but constricting, threatening to suck her in, to hold her down and drown her."[17]

Nabilah is rendered much like a heroine in English colonial fiction; thrown into a suffocating "wilderness" but required to submit to the "heat, dust and sunlight of her husband's untamed land" due to the upward mobility that it provides her.[18] Both wives have two children each, and while they remain equally devoted to providing love and care for their children, their ways of mothering are certainly very different. Waheeba is earthy and open, and she uses food as her language of love. Nabilah is communicative and intellectual, ensuring that her children read books and excel in education.

Neither is particularly palatable characters, and it is the moving journey of Mahmoud's son Nur and his love story with Soraya that tethers the readers to the novel. Positioning these two women in such a manner, however, does unmask Leila's way of approaching her own half-Sudanese and half-Egyptian identity. Despite a well-drawn-out, deep and complex picture of Nabilah, and even with Waheeba's shockingly inappropriate and violent event of forcing Nabilah's daughter to genital cutting, it is Sudan and the Sudanese that prevail within the representation. Waheeba, who comes from wealth and business connections, is a step up for Mahmoud in his years as a struggling youth, whereas Nabilah represents a late-stage love affair, and a vain conquest predicated upon his wealth and power.

Lyrics Alley is Leila's first historical novel that draws from actual Aboulela family history with regard to the story of Nur but fills out the narrative through a fictionalized representation of the life and intimate politics of the Omdurman saraya. The character of Nabilah consolidates many of Leila's observations about how Egyptians felt about Sudan, and her own mother's sense of not quite fitting into the life of the Sudanese saraya is also depicted with sympathy and sensitivity. The novel is, after all, about the last days of Egyptian Sudan, and uses the family plot to allegorize the structural difficulties within the Sudanese and Egyptian relationship, while trying to assert a Sudanese way forward. This path may never be fully free of Egyptian influence, but there is clarity about the attachment and commitment to a cultural and personal identity that remains distinctly Sudanese.

Egyptian mothers return in *Minaret* with Lamya and her mother Doctora Zeinab, who employ Najwa to care for Lamya's daughter, Mai, in London. The tight-knit trio replicates Leila's year in London, with her husband out of town and Mona stepping in to help with her first baby so that Leila could continue her master's studies. Though it is not emphasized much in the novel, Doctora Zeinab tells Najwa that Lamya was born in Khartoum, and that her father is Sudanese. Perhaps this detail is meant to worry Najwa since her family has a notorious reputation, or perhaps to generate a stronger connection for her, but it does appear that Leila is not able to detangle from the structure of the Sudanese father and Egyptian mother.

Lamya is presented as a mirroring character for Najwa: the picture of empowerment, independence, and affluence, while Najwa chooses the religious route in hopes of building her life after several tragic circumstances. In this scenario, Doctora Zeinab is the quintessential matriarch. Najwa welcomes her firm hand and steady stewarding as she takes care of Mai and does household duties. While Lamya may not necessarily appreciate her mother, Najwa finds relief and peace in the submission that the matriarch and employer demands of her, thus consolidating yet again the thread of domineering and strong mothers alongside their less self-assured daughters.

These recurring patterns in Leila's oeuvre are impossible to ignore, pointing to the fact that Leila's own relationship with her mother is one of the most significant, complex and poignant attachments in her life. The other is her long and enduring relationship with her husband, Nadir, whom she met as a young adolescent. Romance, love, and the marriage plot are important and overarching themes in Leila's fiction. Tangled within her attachment-oriented worldview is also her preoccupation with faith, Islam, and finding love and solace in God, which too can be traced to a parallel period of Khartoum girlhood that will be explored in detail in the next chapter.

Notes

1 Modern Sudan (@DocomomoSD), "Building of the Week," Facebook, November 19, 2022, https://www.facebook.com/DocomomoSD/posts/building-of-the-week-the-abulelaa-complex-is-one-of-sudans-earliest-modern-build/132464986276026/
2 Wikimedia, "Khartoum-ShariaGamhurria-AboulelaBuilding," last modified September 23, 2025, https://commons.wikimedia.org/wiki/File:Khartoum-ShariaGamhurria-AboulelaBuilding_RomanDeclert17022013.jpg
3 Eulogy to Floyce Abdelwahab, Facebook post, February 16, 2016. https://www.facebook.com/laboulela
4 Leila Aboulela, "Baby love," *Wasafiri*, vol. 19, no. 42, 121–124. https://doi.org/10.1080/02690050408589926
5 Leila Aboulela, "Baby love," *Wasafiri*, vol. 19, no. 42, 122.
6 Leila Aboulela (@laboulela), "Eulogy to Floyce Abdelwahab," Facebook, February 16, 2016, https://www.facebook.com/photo/?fbid=661364547300368&set=a.146246015478893
7 "Leila Aboulela visits her old school in Khartoum 2008," filmed by Taghred Elsanhouri in 2008, video by BBC – Encounters, posted by Leila Fuad, YouTube, posted on Oct 13, 2013, https://www.youtube.com/watch?v=ZekJ13_g3rU
8 Leila Aboulela, "Farida's Eyes" in *Elsewhere, Home* (Black Cat, an imprint of Grove Atlantic: 2019), 51.
9 Leila Aboulela, "The Boy from the Kebab Shop," in *Coloured Lights* (Polygon: 2001), 60.

10 Leila Aboulela, "Tuesday Lunch" in *Coloured Lights* (Polygon: 2001), 81.
11 Leila Aboulela, "Make Your Own Way Home," in *Coloured Lights* (Polygon: 2001), 84.
12 Leila Aboulela, *The Translator* (Grove Atlantic: 2006), 7.
13 Leila Aboulela, *Lyrics Alley* (Phoenix/Orion Books: 2010), 16.
14 Leila Aboulela, *Lyrics Alley* (Phoenix/Orion Books: 2010), 16.
15 Leila Aboulela, *Lyrics Alley* (Phoenix/Orion Books: 2010), 29.
16 Leila Aboulela, *Lyrics Alley* (Phoenix/Orion Books: 2010), 9.
17 Leila Aboulela, *Lyrics Alley* (Phoenix/Orion Books: 2010), 24.
18 Leila Aboulela, *Lyrics Alley* (Phoenix/Orion Books: 2010), 24.

3 Love and Faith, Faith and Love

"It was a good relationship and Nadir is a very nice person. But there were differences that he and his family did not understand. Because I am Arab and Muslim, I was thinking of marriage, everything has to do with marriage."

Mona Khalifa laughed as she explained her logic behind the precise direction her 17-year-old daughter Leila's relationship with her 19-year-old boyfriend Nadir Mahjoub should have been taking. Leila had been seeing Nadir for almost two years, and even though there was approval from both sets of parents, Mona believed that it was time to make it official. Fuad thought his wife was being over the top and did not approve of pressuring his teenage daughter to commit to marriage. Nadir's parents protested too and rightfully asserted that their children were simply too young. But Mona insisted that solidifying their commitment would give them the freedom to be seen together and to spend time without the judgmental, prying eyes of the social circles they belonged to.

As usual, Mona got her way, and the Aboulelas hosted a modest engagement party at their home in February 1982. It was a small gathering; tea and snacks were served, and family elders were in attendance. Photos of the casual after-party in the living room capture a tall and slender Leila looking radiant in a bright pink, sleeveless V-neck dress. Her hair is a short halo of curls, and the only jewelry she wears is a simple beaded necklace.

After the more formal rituals were concluded, Nadir and Leila went on to jointly cut a two-tiered cake with white frosting, as family members milled around. It was a happy and intimate occasion, but it would be a full three years before the teen sweethearts would get married, and even after that, their relationship would have to survive several long-distance iterations, a difficult migration to London, and then to Aberdeen. However, for Leila, who went on to become a successful writer, it was at this

DOI: 10.4324/9781003306719-4

time that the seeds of her knowledge about love, marriage and religion were sown.

***

A studious routine

At age 14, three years before her engagement, Leila was a bespectacled teenager with plump cheeks and an open smile. She sported the same haircut as her entire class—curly layers with a few short tendrils falling over the forehead—a trend that had gripped Khartoum. She had settled into a comfortable social and domestic routine with friends at the Sisters School and the American Club.

The social and academic parts of her schooling came easily, and Leila also thrived in the strictness of the religious structure. The nuns, with their austere affect, flowing religious robes, and covered heads, made a resounding impression on her. In a filmed return to the school in 2008, Leila spent some time in the shaded spot on the playground where a small Ave Maria chapel is located. "To me, it was a symbol of beauty," she explained, adding that she found "the sisters were very beautiful in what they were wearing, and they were inspiring for me. I thought that they were very strong and that they had made a sacrifice."[1] Faith, she discovered, also had an aesthetic, and it pleased Leila and inspired a sense of marvel and serenity in her. Even though it was too early for her to start deepening her own faith, the seeds seemed to have been planted in her mind during those years at the Catholic girls' school.

Studious and hardworking, Leila excelled at academics, but she also read voraciously and lightly dabbled in playing the piano. With a set of friends at the Sisters School and at the American School, and regular visits to the saraya in Omdurman, Leila's social calendar was more than full. Mona had completed her PhD in London by then and returned to resume her life and career back in Khartoum. In reprising her role as full-time mother, Mona's main concern was Leila receiving the best high school diploma possible, so that she would have strong chances to go to a ranked university and pursue any desired career options. She had to make a choice between the British system and the Sudanese system, which would be entirely in Arabic. Mona chose the difficult route and decided that her daughter—and eventually also Khalid—would sit for the Sudanese high school exams.

Preparations began in earnest three years in advance. With Leila only proficient in colloquial Arabic and the Quran, and with schooling at the Sisters School continuing as usual, Mona added a tutor to improve both her children's proficiency in Arabic. Unsurprisingly, the tutor was an Egyptian man who taught at the Egyptian school in Khartoum, and a dedicated Mona would drive over, pick him up and drop him back every afternoon. Not only were the two teenagers under pressure to improve their Arabic, but the Egyptian tutor was also under pressure to gain fluency in the Sudanese curriculum.

Still, there remained one outstanding problem. Leila's Arabic was improving in leaps and bounds, but the exams would still require her to prepare all the subjects—mathematics, geography, sciences, literature, and grammar in Arabic—disciplines she only knew in English. Mona found a particularly labor-intensive solution. Perhaps inspired by her own maternal grandfather's penchant for translating Dickens' novels from English to Arabic, she put Leila to the task of translating all her Arabic textbooks into English, thus killing two birds with one stone: not only was Leila inadvertently studying for the exams, but she was also making herself an expert in two curricula in two languages.

Some of this activity took place during school holidays, which the Aboulelas had started to spend in London. After Mona's long London stint, Fuad decided to purchase a pied-à-terre for the family. While Mona ran around, working on her research and publications, Leila was installed in the university library, where she spent hours on her textbook translation exercise. Mona contributed by translating many of the science textbooks for both her children, leaving the humanities texts to Leila. Over 50 years later, Mona could recall jointly translating the history textbook about the Mahdist war in 19th-century Sudan, which would become the base for Leila's historical novel *River Spirit.*

The madness certainly had a method, and it all paid off. Leila ranked 7th in nationwide exam results, and Mona was flush with pride. Mistakes made with the under-rigorous American school were finally rectified; first, with switching schools from the American school to the Sisters School, and then eventually culminating in an extraordinary practice of translations for the exams. "It had all come together," Mona beamed.

Without a doubt, Leila was exceptionally gifted at academics, and she never complained, no matter how irrational the tasks set forth by her mother. Much of this came easily for her, and she enjoyed discipline, rigor, and routine. It centered her and gave her purpose. However, her grueling academic schedule did not deter her from the typical social life of a bourgeois Khartoum teenager. Soon enough, evenings at the American club took on a whole new significance when she laid eyes on Nadir Ahmed Mahjoub. A couple of years older and a student at the Comboni school for boys, Nadir's bright eyes, angular face, and cavalier confidence exuded a magnetic charm. He knew of Leila as they ran in the same circles, but it took quite a while before he came to reciprocate her feelings.

The Mahjoubs

Nadir was not a natural fit with the wealthy and traditional Aboulela business family. His father, Ahmed Mahjoub, was a self-made man who hailed from very humble circumstances in Bahri in northern Khartoum. His oldest son, Jamal, who went on to become a prolific writer, wrote that his father was "born in a house of mud bricks" and "received only a rudimentary education."[2] Having lost his own father before he was even born, and raised by various relatives, Ahmed Mahjoub knew from a young age that he would have to make his own path in life. Though he did not have the opportunity for formal education, he was skilled in languages and soon acquired fluency in English. What he lacked in connections, he made up for in street smarts and strong people skills. As a young man, he worked in a library and continued to improve his English.

Ahmed was charming and fashionable, with a talent for regaling people with stories. And, thanks to his fluency in English, he found himself in London in the early fifties. He had secured a job as a student liaison at the Sudanese embassy and was responsible for Sudanese citizens arriving in the UK to pursue higher education. A work romance soon blossomed between him and Judith Gerlach, a young woman from London.

The daughter of a German father and English mother, Judith was attractive with an aquiline nose and high cheekbones. She was unique because she had a genuine curiosity about the world and an interest in languages, art, literature, and culture. Judith stood quite a few inches taller than Ahmed, and teenage Leila remembers finding the couple to be rather shocking and unconventional to look at. Judith was a voracious reader and, being just as skilled as Ahmed in languages, she was making rapid headway in Arabic. Judith's father did not warm to the idea of his daughter marrying a Black man from Africa, but the couple was certain of their commitment to each other. The two were married in 1955, "breaking 'centuries of taboo': a black man marrying a white woman."[3]

Ahmed found a job as a branch manager with the Gezira Scheme, now a well-established and lucrative agricultural industry focused primarily on cotton to be exported to Europe. The young couple moved to Sudan and spent a few years in Barakat in Wad Medani, before returning to London. Given his English language skills, Ahmed was asked to manage the arrival of Sudanese cotton to the UK. Their first son, Jamal, was born in 1960, and this was soon followed by a move to Liverpool to be closer to the port where the cotton from Sudan arrived. Ahmed and Judith entered a hectic, but happy parenting phase. Nadir was born on May 14, 1962, and two years later, another boy, Akram, was born.

Nadir recalls a normal childhood, boisterous even, with three active boys running around. Yet, it was the sixties, and this was an unusual family composed of a Black Muslim man, a white English woman, and their three interracial children. More than Nadir, it is Jamal whose writing career went on to engage in honest and unsparing reflections on the experiences of racism and xenophobia in a conservative England. This was a time of immense tumult for the British as their massive empire was coming apart at the seams, with various countries in Africa decolonizing and gaining independence. Sudan itself had just acquired autonomy, and in a way, men like Ahmed were part of a generation that was actively building the nation, whether by working in the embassy or being part of developing the Gezira scheme. Young Nadir knew they were different, but Judith was their portal for gaining entry into the white and English world. For the most part, the children moved in and out of those spaces easily. Their father kept the Sudanese connection alive by socializing with the few Sudanese families that had moved to the UK.

After almost a decade of living in the UK, the Mahjoubs moved back to Sudan, this time to Khartoum. Ahmed had gained a sterling reputation as a business manager and was offered a job to facilitate the installation of the manufacturing giant, Caterpillar, in Sudan.

For the seven-year-old Nadir, the move felt transformative and freeing. The constant sunshine and easy conviviality were a drastic change from the cold, soggy Liverpool weather. "There was this sudden feeling that you're living your life outdoors under the sun, under the wind, and the clear skies and stars everywhere." Nadir explained that "your senses are suddenly woken up." Inherently social, popular, and with a proclivity for fun, Nadir found it to be a time of unfettered sociality with groups of friends, as the comings and goings with the kids were easy in the up-and-coming affluent family neighborhood of Nimra in Khartoum.

With Ahmed consumed with Caterpillar, Judith first started working as a secretary at the university but then went on to set up her own business. Ahmed had diabetes, and Judith also tended to struggle with her weight, so she set up Khartoum's first-ever Diabetic Food Center, a shop that sold food products with low or no sugar. In 2007, Jamal wrote an essay dedicated to his mother and bemusedly asks, "How my parents had come up with the idea of opening a shop I will never know. For as long as I could remember, it had been a source of domestic strife. Right from the start it seemed fated to fail."[4] Certainly, it did not fail, but it underwent many additions and makeovers. Sugar-free goods were an untapped corner of the market since there was nothing else like it for Sudanese with diabetes. Luxury items such as jams, biscuits, and juices made with fruit sugar, and whole meal flour were the staple of the little storefront, with all the items imported from the UK.

At some point, Judith also added on a "slimming center" at the back of the store. On a practical level, this might have been a way to gain more traction for the business, but it seemed typical of Judith to be *au courant* with goings-on in the UK. She acquired the certification for training people on the Slendertone machines, which were extremely popular in the US and the UK during the seventies and eighties. Powered by electricity, the machines required users to put on protective pads as belts vibrated at high speed to trim fat from targeted body parts. The shop acquired one such machine, which Jamal described as "our star attraction." Jamal had a mean-spirited description of the demographic of the customers: "Khartoum was full of affluent ladies worried that their husbands might lose interest in them long enough to find themselves a younger, slimmer wife." He added that the "bulky women would squeeze through the narrow gap and disappear into the shaded booth."[5] But they "never looked any less plump when they emerged, and so it was perhaps not surprising that their husbands tended to grow tired of paying for treatment that had no discernible diminishing effect on anything but their wallets."[6] Nevertheless, Jamal writes that this shop had become "something of a refuge for strangers;" many of whom would be expatriate wives looking to shoot the breeze or people looking for a respite from the afternoon heat.

Without doubt, the slimming-center-plus-diet-goods shop was quite popular, and it was a busy and productive time for the Mahjoubs. The store was a family affair, and the boys were occasionally roped into working there. Some days, they would end up at the shop after school and wait until their mother closed it so they could be driven back home.

The business was a huge success until political instability started to become a permanent feature of the country. Gafaar Nimeiri had taken power in 1969 and implemented an ambitious scheme "to turn Sudan into a regional 'breadbasket.'" In 1977, he launched a six-year plan to bring more than six million feddans (6.2 million acres) into cultivation. This project had two goals: to guarantee Sudan's food security, and to produce animal products and grain for export to the Arab world.[7] Yet the overcultivation of monocrops, expropriation of land from farmers and pastoralists, and a devastating drought meant that Nimeiri borrowed heavily from international actors and plunged the country into crippling debt. While Khartoum and its elite did not experience the immediate effects of these policies at first, the discontent gradually began to spread through student and civil unrest.

Businesses also started to feel the impact of tightened restrictions and exorbitant customs and duties on imports. Judith found it hard to stay in business and turned her attention to local art. She repurposed the store into a gallery plus shop for local arts, textiles, clothing, and artifacts. Over time, she even took to making her own jewelry using Sudanese stones and materials. In 1989, there was yet another coup. Omar Al-Bashir began consolidating power and became the dictator of Sudan for the next three decades. Anticipating that Sudan would never be the same again, Ahmed and Judith decided to leave Khartoum and carved out a life shuttling between London and Cairo.

The three boys were enrolled in Comboni College, the Catholic boys-only equivalent of the Sisters School. Nadir's academic trajectory was the opposite of Leila's. He did not exactly fail out of class but slid by year after year with the bare minimum, passing marks. In a way, older brother Jamal cast a long shadow, being both academically talented and a voracious reader like their mother Judith. Akram also did rather well at school. But no one was particularly worried about Nadir, who tended to expend his energy on sports. He participated, for example, in the absurdly dangerous fire ring jump, par for the course in the overly energetic environment of the all-boys school. The fire ring jump competition was held on the Comboni annual sports day, attended by students from the other Khartoum schools. Leila remembers lining up to see Nadir, her crush, jump through the hoop of fire in the gymnastics challenge.

It took some time before Nadir took notice of the serious and studious Leila. Though the Mahjoub family had access to the British country club, the pool and the burgers at the American Club often won out for mixed or expat families, and so it was as much Nadir's stomping ground as Leila's. The families knew of each other since the American Club members and their children were, after all, a small clique with overlapping, intersecting lives. Naturally flirtatious and likable, Nadir was also known to be seeing other girls. Since Nadir did not reciprocate Leila's feelings just yet, she navigated her crush on him with a sense of immense turmoil. Often, high-strung, passionate dramas ensued among the gossipy gang of girlfriends to ensure that no secret information about Leila's feelings, or her views on one of Nadir's girlfriends, would leak out.

Sarah Abdelaziz, a close friend from the American Club days, laughingly recalls the two girls playing the cheesy Bee Gees hit from 1977, "How Deep Is Your Love" over and over, and Leila practicing the theme soundtrack of the film *Love Story* on the piano. She also indulged in a steady diet of widely available paperbacks that included romantic fiction from Mills and Boon, especially their most prolific author, Denise Robins, as well as historical romances by Jean Plaidy. Leila was neither prone to overt displays of affection nor grand declarations, but she certainly had a romantic side and even dabbled in writing some stories. But this was a sporadic activity, and possibly an outlet for a teenager straddling an intensely studious routine and an unrequited crush.

For Nadir, Leila was in a league of her own and perhaps intimidating, because of her quiet and observant persona. But she also had a familiar bookishness that Nadir associated with his mother and older brother. He was drawn to her "air of intelligence," and realized that Leila had a depth that made her unique. To a degree, she was also the most mysterious of the girls at the American club because she was reserved and did not draw attention to herself. Even though Nadir knew about her family and had encountered her brother Khalid, he had had no direct contact with Leila. Over time, however, they began chatting with each other, first in a group and then taking walks on the club grounds, just the two of them. "People were running around playing catch or playing basketball. And we would be just walking through this at a steady pace," Nadir conjures a picture in his mind, "through this commotion all around." Leila represented a necessary calm for Nadir's much busier mind, and commotion within. She had a soothing influence on him.

These were difficult days for Nadir. He had taken his O-level exams, and his marks fell short of gaining him entrance to the University of Khartoum. Parents and friends of the family started scrambling to ensure that he could enroll at a university, perhaps in Morocco, perhaps in rural Sudan. It did not help that his older brother Jamal was already doing particularly well academically. A long, heartfelt conversation with Leila during this stressful moment marked a turning point for Nadir. Leila listened, always understood, and anchored him. From that moment on, the connection deepened slowly and soon enough, Nadir and Leila were "going steady."

Leila admits that while teenagers often experience coming of age by rebelling against their parents and breaking out of family structures, she was extremely focused on her own love story, which to her could have

Figure 3.1 Leila and Nadir, Khartoum, 1982

only one desirable outcome: marriage. “I wanted to marry this very young man, who didn’t have a job, he didn’t have a university degree. A lot of my creativity, a lot of my time and energy went into that.” Not only had she expended enormous amounts of time and “creativity” into being in love, giving it shape, and finding a trajectory for it, she believes that she “saw the world through that.”

Love and marriage as literature

Love came to have a very particular place in Leila’s fiction once she located herself as a writer; but that vocation was distant and unfamiliar to the teenager, still 15 years away. Desire, love, marriage and religion are often intricately and deliberately entwined in Leila’s fiction, and the experience of love, whether fulfilled or unrequited, becomes a necessary vehicle for growth and self-realization for her women protagonists.

The Translator relies upon the enduring fictional trope of the “marriage plot” defined by scholars of English literature as “any narrative that ends, or almost ends, in a marriage or marriages and that is largely concerned throughout with courtship.”[8] Nancy Armstrong has argued that “stories of courtship and marriage offered their readers a way of indulging, with a kind of impunity, in fantasies of political power that were the more acceptable because they were played out within a domestic framework.”[9] In this way, such stories asserted political power without appearing to contest its fundamental structure and the monogamous marriage allowed for the structure of female subordination to the male to be affirmed.

Leila is open about being influenced by these precise English novels that she read voraciously as a teenager. She found the “courtship rituals” in a Jane Austen novel to be “romantic and refreshing, innocence surviving today’s tumultuous, often difficult reality.”[10]

The Translator fits rather neatly into this category and tells the story of Sudanese widow Sammar, who falls in love with the Scottish scholar Rae. There is but one hurdle to their courtship: religion, more specifically, Islam. Though Rae is culturally fluent in the history and politics of Islam and Muslim regions, the novel’s plot hinges on whether Rae will convert or not. Sammar’s political power is shaped over time as their courtship plays out.

Rae is a white, educated male with a powerful position at the university. Indeed, he belongs to the ruling class, and passages throughout the novel expose the extent to which Sammar occupies a marginalized position in Scotland as a Muslim and as a migrant.

Though love and romance bridge some of the differences between Sammar and Rae, marriage to a Muslim man is the only way that she can continue being with him. Leila explained in an interview that

> Sammar is very much the Sudanese "girl next door," typical in her attachment to religious tradition. To ask Rae to convert to Islam in order to marry her is a daring thing to do, but for her it is the only way their love can continue. A relationship outside of marriage is, for her, not an option.[11]

Though the novel refuses to attribute assertive characteristics to Sammar, Rae's eventual conversion not only allows them to be together, but it is also a political victory in an unequally structured and ubiquitously Christian West that practices hostility toward its Muslim and migrant population.

In the years that follow, her fiction takes a much darker, perhaps a more political turn, and in *Minaret*, love is thwarted more than once for Najwa. It is only within the deepening of her faith that she finds solace. Unlike in *The Translator*, love is a failed pursuit in *Minaret*, and religion supplants the desire for romance and companionship.

The University Years

It took a village to sort out Nadir's university crisis. Parents and friends of the family started scrambling to ensure that he could enroll at a university and came upon the option of the University of Gezira, established in 1975 in Wad Medani. It was a new initiative spearheaded by President Nimeiry himself and offered an American-style education with grade point averages (GPAs) and a semester system. Nadir filled out the application and was soon on his way. With decent grades in mathematics and an interest in engineering and mechanics, Nadir was on track at the Faculty of Science and Technology. But a bubble had suddenly burst; the casual comfort of the parental home and the Khartoum he knew like the back of his hand was now gone. Nadir was living on his own for the first time, almost three hours away.

There were other challenges. Nadir found himself in an all-Arabic environment, which was different from the English he was accustomed to speaking at home and at school. Also, commuting back and forth to Khartoum was not very easy. Buses were the only mode of transport, and they often broke down or took six hours instead of three. But Sudan, the country, also revealed itself to him, with students from different parts of the country commingling and living together in hostels. It was a world radically different from the small, elite Khartoum scene. Unbeknownst to

Nadir, it was also a preview into the life of long, isolated stints on oil rigs in remote locations that his career would lead him to.

By the time Leila was 16 years old, her special friendship with Nadir was evident to most people, despite her generally private and muted demeanor about it. Around this time, the couple also made it official for themselves. And eventually, Leila told her mother about it. It was not entirely clear whether Leila sought her mother's approval, or whether she needed Mona to give the final push that might make the relationship official, scheming toward a marriage of her own. Nadir was two years older after all and was soon to leave school and enter a different phase of his life. Perhaps there were aspects of his less-traditional parents and his effervescent, flirtatious personality that worried Leila; or perhaps she wondered if he might slip away. The engagement, planned at Mona's command, did away with any such anxieties and uncertainties.

Leila and Nadir were now engaged and met as often as it was possible for Nadir to visit. Leila was immersed in her studies and focused on preparing for her challenging exams. Nadir was moving along in his studies in Gezira, but civil unrest in Sudan was increasing, and student protests led to universities sending their students home for days on end as negotiations with student unions would be touch-and-go, often stalled for months. After two and a half years of these instabilities, Nadir and his family started to think about other options.

"Another upheaval," Nadir called it when it was decided that the American University of Cairo would be his next academic stop. Completely unlike Leila's family, Nadir had no familiarity with Egypt at all, and Cairo was bustling and chaotic, "an exponential learning curve." He had to get used to Egyptian Arabic, fend for himself in a foreign country, and navigate the busy and alienating city using public transport. In the university's American system, there was constant debate about which Gezira credits could transfer, and Nadir was pushed back almost to the start. But he had a focus now to get himself a real career.

Though he did not see Leila too often during those years, his commitment to the marriage played a part in pushing him to succeed at university. In a way, Leila was woven into the fabric of his daily life too, since he was living in Mona's parents' empty flat in Cairo and in the final year of college, his roommate was Leila's younger brother, Khalid. He worked tirelessly, taking extra credits and keeping up a good GPA, and graduated with a major in physics, with a specialization in solid-state electronics.

Back in Khartoum, Leila passed her exams with flying colors and secured admission to the University of Khartoum for a major in Economics with a specialization in Statistics. Due to Mona's machinations during Leila's early school years, Leila was two years ahead in her educational trajectory, having skipped some grades in her transition from the American School to the Sisters School. This meant she was only a year behind

Nadir, and they were entering their university phases somewhat simultaneously. Everything was going as planned; Leila was on track for a potential academic career similar to her mother's, she was engaged and secure in the relationship with Nadir, and Nadir himself was becoming mature, and had begun to take stock of his own life and career back in Cairo.

For Leila, the happy yet cloistered spaces of her Khartoum girlhood were replaced by the vibrancy of university life. The main campus of the university in central Khartoum was beautiful, with wide avenues flanked by palm trees. The red, brick-colored buildings blended English colonial architecture along with Arab and Sudanese elements, such as pointed arches for doors and windows. Trim green lawns lined the various two or three-storied buildings of the various faculties and departments, and the library, at almost 2000 square meters, was one of the largest and most important in Sudan.

Leila was immersed in her life at the university while getting to know different members of the Mahjoub family. Akram, Nadir's younger brother, was enrolled in the Architecture program at the same university, and the two became close. After the engagement, the Mahjoubs and Aboulelas would visit each other often. Leila remembers Judith coming by on Saturdays, and she attributes a host of different influences to her future mother-in-law, seeing Judith as distilling into Leila and her family a sort of worldliness.

Figure 3.2 Leila placed 7th in nationwide exams and received a certificate from the president of Sudan, Gaafar Nimeiry

Life thus far was lived with the rigorous Egyptian-ness inculcated by Mona and the comfortable Sudanese-ness of her father's side of the family. Despite the Aboulelas' financial capacity to take holidays in London, Judith's lifestyle and interests were more fluid and cosmopolitan, and she moved easily between cultures and embraced the new. The two families ended up meeting in London, and Leila was surprised, for example, when Judith chose an Afghan restaurant one time, and a vegetarian one at a different time. Her inherent openness and rather unique way of navigating the city appealed to Leila, and it was an influence that Leila came to lean on during the early, alienating years of her migration to the UK.

Leila did not aspire, in her wildest dreams, to become a writer, the mere idea far too distant at this time. But with Judith in her life, a whole new world of reading opened itself to her. Judith read widely and introduced Leila to the feminist Virago modern classics series founded in 1973. The series was composed of new publications and reprints of older books, and its range was vast, with literary works by the likes of Edith Wharton, Antonia White, Eudora Welty and Angela Carter, and writers who tread the line between genre fiction and literature, such as Daphne du Maurier, Patricia Highsmith, Joyce Carol Oates and Ursula LeGuin.[12]

Judith also liked reading books by winners of the Booker Prize, and this led Leila to writers from the postcolonial Commonwealth. Memorably, Leila remembers that during Judith's final days battling skin cancer in a nursing home in 1998, she was reading *Sula* by Toni Morrison. But Judith was not simply thrusting heavy literary works in Leila's hands. She also bought her *Vogue* magazine when Leila was trying to pick out wedding dresses. Between them, there was a relaxed intimacy, and Leila was a willing recipient of Judith's affection; perhaps she even had a penchant for attracting mother figures.

Judith, too, seemed just as willing to embrace her future daughter-in-law, and Leila benefited from being the only significant young woman to frequent the Mahjoub home, since neither Jamal nor Akram had introduced any significant others to the family. Judith died in 1998, one year before Leila's debut novel *The Translator* was published. But in the years right until her death, Judith was a strong presence in Leila's life as she settled in the UK, had three children and began writing. In fact, Judith "was to become her internal audience," Leila said in an interview.[13]

As with Nadir in Gezira, years at the university suddenly exposed different sides of Sudan to Leila. The university comprised an incredible array of students from different class and race backgrounds from many different parts of Sudan. But there was something else too; an attraction to the more religious and traditional Sudanese girls from the provinces who studied at the university. Leila explained:

> I grew up in Khartoum in a very westernized, secular community (even though my mother had a lot of faith inside her). The schools I

> went to were a private American school and then a Catholic missionary school where none of the girls wore hijab; they wouldn't dream of doing so. But when I went to university, I suddenly encountered students from the provinces who were veiled and very religious, and that made an impact on me.[14]

Indeed, modest religious clothing and veiling were frowned upon among the Khartoum elite, and there was a commitment to look and dress Western, be fluent in English, and be more or less comfortable with Western customs and socialization.

Mona was certainly religious, and Leila had grown up with both her mother and her Egyptian grandmother instilling a sense of faith and spirituality in her. And for them, being religious was not in contradiction with being educated, progressive, and having a career. With a grandmother who studied medicine in the forties, and a mother who was a university professor, Leila's "idea of religion wasn't about a woman not working or having to dress in a certain way; it was more to do with the faith," she clarified.[15] Even though religion and faith were fairly ingrained in Leila, she was drawn to the girls at the university in a sort of aesthetic way, and found within herself a proclivity toward the beauty in piety, and an attraction to the beautiful, white flowing "tobes." This was also not a new feeling; rather, it seemed to be a rekindling of the pleasure that this aesthetic had brought her as a young girl, surrounded by nuns in their flowing frocks and habits at the Sisters School.

The university was plagued with various strikes, and civil unrest was a common feature at the time; and there existed a small but vocal feminist movement. The Sudanese Women's Union (SWU) was founded in 1952 and had held its inaugural meeting on the university grounds in the years that would lead up to Sudanese independence.[16] The Sudanese Women's Union (SWU) was a formidable group and participated in various protests and revolutions in the ensuing decades, often drawing members from the female student bodies at the universities and vocational institutes. But by the seventies, SWU was forcefully dismantled. The work, however, had taken root, and women's demonstrations continued, with causes ranging from the release of political prisoners to the high cost of living. During the eighties, women were not only members of political parties, but there was also a broader awareness about their social and political rights.[17]

A lot of this feminist activism naturally spilled into campus life, and some of the campus political activity finds its way into her second novel, *Minaret,* where she traces the journey of a privileged Khartoum girl, Najwa, whose family's fall from grace leaves her completely alone, penniless, and unmoored in London. Narrated in the first person, nostalgia for her Khartoum youth is a large component of Najwa's journey toward self-actualization. The novel flashes back and forth in time and moves between Khartoum and London as Najwa unsuccessfully searches for love and financial stability. Religion will be her answer, but this does not come as a surprise because Najwa's attraction to the "provincial girls" at the university is established early in the novel.

When asked about her religious turn in her early twenties, Leila does not hesitate to reveal a strand of autobiography in the novel, and her university anecdote is similar to what Najwa expresses. Early in the novel, Najwa observes two young girls leaving the library:

> They both wore white tobes and one of them was very cute with deep dimples and sparkling eyes. They were provincial girls and I was a girl from the capital and that was the reason we were not friends. With them I felt, for the first time in my life, self-conscious of my clothes; my too short skirts and too tight blouses. Many girls dressed like me, so I was not unusual. Yet these provincial girls made me feel awkward. I was conscious of their modest grace, of the tobes that covered their slimness—pure white cotton covering their arms and hair.[18]

In addition to articulating the schism between the urban and rural populations, Najwa confesses an aesthetic attraction to traditional Muslim and Sudanese clothing. Leila articulated this attraction in many interviews after the novel was published. "I talk about this in *Minaret*: seeing the university girls in their veils, and watching them pray." It can be argued that the university years were formative and eye-opening for Leila in grasping a wide diversity of women's worlds; the inadvertently Western form of feminist empowerment that her group of friends espoused, the more radical and nationalist women student groups active on campus, and the large majority of women students from outside Khartoum that lived their lives and religion in a different way than Leila was used to.

The fascination with tobes continues, and Najwa admiringly scrutinizes the same girls during the evening classes after the girls changed out of their white tobes into colorful ones. Najwa "liked watching the change in them, from the plain white in the morning to blue and pink flowers, patterns in bold colors."[19] In London, as Najwa contemplates everything she lost in Khartoum, she recalls the same girls praying with covered hair who held her still with "their slow movements. I envied them something I didn't have but I didn't know what it was."[20]

As her life plunges into misery in London, Najwa gradually discovers that the missing element in her life was the clear anchor of faith. Slowly, the aesthetic fascination with the sartorial evolves into an embrace of Islam, and Najwa also starts to wear hijab and dress modestly. It takes exile and feeling in intense isolation for Najwa to immerse herself in practices and rituals that she had only fleetingly paid attention to in the past.

Given the similarities between Najwa's character and Leila's own articulation of her faith, it is not far-fetched to argue that the university was a place where some of these stirrings began but were only harnessed after experiencing alienation and homesickness in the UK. Furthermore, Leila's declared intention to keep Khartoum alive and to strive to depict its beauty can be evidenced in descriptions of the university and the quotidian life of young people in the city. Najwa describes the cafeteria that overlooks the Blue Nile, walks taken from the library to various classrooms or the post office, and activist events held on campus in the evenings. In the context of biography, the influence of this university, its politics and its social universe was profound, especially as it became Leila's last lived experience of Khartoum and remained etched in her mind in the years abroad that were to follow.

Wedding in Khartoum

Nadir's plan of studying hard, getting a degree, and securing a job was now in motion. Transferring to the American University of Cairo paid off, as they were able to attract many multinational companies to show up at their job fairs and recruit young graduates. Even before he graduated, Nadir landed a plum position at Schlumberger, one of the world's largest offshore oil drilling companies. Ecstatic that things were finally going according to plan and relieved that all his hard work had paid off, Nadir decided it was time to get married and start a new chapter in his and Leila's life.

The Aboulelas had moved out of their home in Al-Amarat, and had bought a house in the Burri neighborhood, known as Garden City. Mona set about preparing for a large wedding celebration in their new home and its large garden. Ensuring that it took place during cooler weather was important, and Nadir and Leila, ages 23 and 21, respectively, were wed on November 3, 1984, on a Sunday afternoon, with a reception party that carried on into the evening. Almost 200 guests spilled into the house and lawn. The wedding leaned toward Egyptian traditions, with several bridesmaids—all cousins and friends—holding large lighted candles behind the bride and groom.

It was only three years since Lady Diana's extravagant wedding, with her 23-foot train shown on television. It was a dress replicated across the world, and Leila's white wedding gown with layered and voluminous sleeves and a puffy, bouffant skirt was a nod to the fashion of the times. Her short curls were held in place by a simple white headband. Nadir was more modest, in an elegant gray suit accessorized with a shiny off-white tie and cravat. Mona, in a blue satin gown, and Fuad in a light green safari suit were also in line with the fashion trends. The wedding did not incorporate Sudanese customs, but there was no mistaking that this was a fancy Khartoum wedding, with many of the women guests in brightly colored tobes and turbaned men in jalabiyas.

Politically, it was not the easiest of times, with Nimeiri's government on the verge of collapse and an unstable transition ongoing. The wedding had to end by 11:00 pm because of a state-imposed curfew, but that did not dampen the celebrations in any way. Leila and Nadir were happily rushed off for their wedding night to the fancy Friendship Palace Hotel. It was a joyful and memorable occasion, with every member of the large Aboulela clan and the much smaller Mahjoub family in attendance.

The newlyweds took off to London for their honeymoon, but Nadir got a call from his new employers who needed him to go to Indonesia for training. The couple decided to extend their honeymoon and pay out of pocket for Leila to join Nadir in Balikpapan, a port city on Borneo Island, for almost the whole month. Balikpapan was known for oil mining, an industry that Nadir would go on to gain expertise in. Though he had to report to his training duties every day, the couple still saw this as a stroke of luck and made the best of their time in a town populated with beautiful beaches and unique wildlife.

The wedding was the start of a long and loving marriage, but it would be several years before Leila and Nadir would settle into a normal family routine. Nadir's job required him to be away on offshore drilling sites for several weeks at a time. Leila first carried on with her usual Khartoum life, then joined him in the UK, marking the start of a voyage that would rupture everything she had ever known and aspired to. The long periods of isolation in a country decidedly hostile to Muslims and migrants would also force Leila to confront an avalanche of emotions and longings that would find their more evocative articulation in fiction.

Notes

1 "Leila Aboulela visits her old school in Khartoum 2008," YouTube.
2 Peter D. Smith, "A Line in the River by Jamal Mahjoub review—Khartoum, city of memory," *The Guardian*, March 14, 2019, https://www.theguardian.com/books/2019/mar/14/line-in-the-river-khartoum-city-of-memory-jamal-mahjoub
3 PD Smith, "A Line in the River by Jamal Mahjoub review—Khartoum, city of memory," *The Guardian*, March 14, 2019, https://www.theguardian.com/books/2019/mar/14/line-in-the-river-khartoum-city-of-memory-jamal-mahjoub
4 Jamal Mahjoub, "Salamanca," *Transition*, issue 97, vol. 13, no. 3 (2007), 141.
5 Jamal Mahjoub, "Salamanca," *Transition*, issue 97, vol. 13, no. 3 (2007), 141–142.

6 Jamal Mahjoub, "Salamanca," *Transition*, issue 97, vol. 13, no. 3 (2007), 142.
7 Joshua Craze, Kholood Khair, and Raga Makawi, "Sudan Starves," *The New York Review*, June 23, 2024, https://www.nybooks.com/online/2024/06/23/sudan-starves/
8 Lisa O' Connell, *The Origins of the English Marriage Plot: Literature, Politics and Religion in the Eighteenth Century* (Cambridge University Press: 2019), 1–11.
9 Nancy Armstrong, *Desire and Domestic Fiction: A Political History of the Novel* (Oxford University Press: 1990), 36.
10 Leila Aboulela, 'Restraint? Sure. Oppression? Hardly,' *Washington Post*, July 22, 2009, http://www.washingtonpost.com/wp-dyn/content/article/2007/07/20/AR2007072002147.html
11 Leila Aboulela, "Writing as Spiritual Offering: A Conversation with Leila Aboulela," interview by Keija Parssinen, *World Literature Today*, Winter 2020, https://www.worldliteraturetoday.org/2020/winter/writing-spiritual-offering-conversation-leila-aboulela-keija-parssinen
12 "The Complete Virago Modern Classic Collection," *Virago*, https://www.virago.co.uk/imprint/lbbg/virago/page/virago-modern-classic-collection/
13 Malika Browne, "Deviation from the Mean: The Move That Gave Leila Aboulela Something to Write About," *The National News*, January 26, 2021, https://www.thenationalnews.com/mena/arab-showcase/2021/11/11/deviation-from-the-mean-the-move-that-gave-leila-aboulela-something-to-write-home-about/
14 Catherine E. Rashid. "Islamic Individualism and the Logic of the Narrative: An Interview with Leila Aboulela," *Interventions*, vol. 14, no. 4 (2012), 617.
15 Anita Sethi, "Keep the faith," *The Guardian*, June 4, 2005, https://www.theguardian.com/books/2005/jun/05/fiction.features2
16 Elena Vezzadini, "Emancipation through the Press: The Women's Movement and its Discourses on the 'Women's Problem' in Sudan on the Eve of Independence (1950–1956)," in *Ordinary Sudan, 1504–2019: From Social History to Politics from Below Volume 1*, eds. by Elena Vezzadini, Iris Seri-Hersch, Lucie Revilla, Anaël Poussier and Mahassin Abdul Jalil (De Gruyter: 2023), 166.
17 Safa Mohamed Kheir Osman, "Sudanese Women's Participation in the December 2018 Revolution: Historical Roots and Mobilisation Patterns," in *Ordinary Sudan, 1504–2019*, 65–66.
18 Leila Aboulela, *Minaret* (Grove Atlantic: 2005), 14–15.
19 Leila Aboulela, *Minaret* (Grove Atlantic: 2005), 42.
20 Leila Aboulela, *Minaret* (Grove Atlantic: 2005), 134.

4 Sudan Lost

The Voyage Out

"I carried copies of Tayeb Salih's *The Wedding of Zein* and Zeinab Belail's *The Choice* everyday on the bus in London. These books were my homesickness, like holding a warm pebble."

It was the autumn of 1987, and these were Leila's early days as a master's student of statistics at the London School of Economics. Nadir was posted to an offshore oil drilling site in Yemen, and their first baby, Kareem, was yet to turn one. Mona had stepped in and set a routine for the three of them: two academic mothers and a baby. Leila had to attend lectures every day, but her mother had procured a fellowship for herself and had a more flexible schedule. Every morning, Leila took bus number 13 from the apartment near Regent's Park, for about half an hour. Sometimes she read from the two books she carried, sometimes she just held them.

At home, Mona organized all her own study materials on the dining table, and as soon as Kareem went down for a nap, she put the kettle on, made herself some coffee, and worked for a few hours. Not only did Leila learn to replicate this system after she was a mother of three and had become a well-known writer, but she also laid out in detail this small, melancholic, and hermetically sealed universe of the trio in *Minaret*, Leila's only London novel.

The routine went like clockwork, but Leila's emotional state was far from regulated. The university courses were difficult, and the rainy, overcast days felt unending; she missed Khartoum terribly. Motherhood was new and complicated, and they had no luck finding a babysitter for Kareem. Despite her mother's help, it was lonely without Nadir, and all she remembers were bleak days of struggle.

As time passed, the feeling that the stay in the UK was temporary and that return to Khartoum was imminent began to fade, and with that, Leila found herself unmoored and in the grip of a profound sense of shock that she was never going to get her life back. And when, over

DOI: 10.4324/9781003306719-5

ten years later, Leila found herself writing fiction, it was this reservoir of tumult and vertiginous homesickness that she began to articulate. Her writing developed a rigorous "sense of place," that slippery, undefinable way in which people, places and the imagination fold into each other in a narrative; these core characteristics in her writing transformed her into a masterful novelist of nostalgia and memory.

* * *

London blues

The excitement of the wedding and the prolonged honeymoon lasting almost two months dissipated. Nadir was away for long spells, and Leila was still living in her own home with her parents. In a way, it felt like nothing had changed. Leila entered a phase of ennui, now aimless and bored after years of having labored to steer the relationship toward its end goal of marriage.

Fuad and Mona had set up an apartment for Leila upstairs in the same house, and Nadir would come and go as work permitted. Practical as always, Mona was not willing to let these feelings of anticlimax fester, nor was she happy to watch her daughter sit around and wait for her husband. But Leila had rushed full throttle into marriage and family life and was pregnant a year later. The couple welcomed baby Kareem in September 1986, and Leila embraced early motherhood with ease and joy. The fuss over the first grandson, the blessings and visits from relatives, was certainly exciting, but with Nadir still away for prolonged periods, normal family life was evading Leila.

Mona was pushing Leila to apply to colleges in London, and Leila relented. She got accepted into the master's program in Statistics at her mother's alma mater, the London School of Economics. Coincidentally, her brother Khalid was also enrolled in a master's program at Imperial College that same year. The Aboulelas already owned a pied-à-terre in the Regent's Park neighborhood from Mona's time at the London School of Economics (LSE). So, in the autumn of 1987, Khalid, Leila, Mona and ten-month-old Kareem squeezed their large and bustling Khartoum life into a small London apartment. And, of course, Nadir and Fuad would also pass through.

To an outsider, all the Aboulelas and a baby Mahjoub crammed into the London apartment might have appeared chaotic, even a little crazy. But within days, Mona had developed a structure for the family. Leila left first thing in the morning, and Mona had baby Kareem on a schedule. In a way, this was Mona's first time being so hands-on with a little baby, and she leaned on everything she had observed with the highly efficient nanny

Husna when Leila was an infant. Fundamentally disciplined and having spent her adulthood successfully juggling children and an academic career, Mona was not fazed by the rhythm of this life, perhaps was even invigorated by it. Proud of her daughter's acceptance to a prestigious university and keen to carve Leila into a mold of herself, Mona embraced her role as mother and grandmother with great gusto and dreamed of great academic success for her daughter.

Leila's mindset could not have been farther from her mother's. Everything felt unpredictable even though every single day was exactly the same. The LSE classes were exceptionally hard. She admitted many years later that she had precisely described the difficulty she had with the coursework in her award-winning story "The Museum," where Shadia, the young statistics student, realizes that the course required a background she did not have.

The sense of doom, an almost physical sense of failure, was overwhelming for Leila. She confided in her mother, but Mona was not sympathetic because she believed that studies were meant to be challenging, and this was simply how it all was. Leila made some friends and enjoyed the company of many of the international students, but she missed Nadir, and she ached for her old life in Sudan.

Interestingly, Leila was also aware of her newfound anonymity and started to wear a hijab within a week of arriving in London. She had tested the waters back in Khartoum, but her father was against it, and her friends were aghast at the thought of Leila choosing to embrace what they viewed as something provincial and unfashionable. But Leila had always longed to wear a hijab and secretly believed that it not only looked beautiful, dreamy and romantic, but also "became convinced of the need to wear it, that this was the right thing to do. It is the correct way of dressing." Mona, the most religious member of their family, certainly did not mind. Leila opted for the square scarf style pinned to the sides into a triangle shape but did not alter the rest of her clothing, nor intensify prayer in any way. Over the years and depending on her social scene, Leila's hijab would undergo various changes in style, from the strict and heavy rectangle wrap to the much lighter, high turban in the later years made popular by Instagram influencers and YouTube tutorials.

The feelings of dread and isolation that Leila associates with those days in London were placated by wearing the hijab, and by always carrying the two works of Sudanese literature, both somehow bringing her a comforting physical and emotional proximity to her beloved Khartoum. Leila's two chosen books, Tayeb Salih's *Wedding of Zein* and Zeinab Belail's *The Choice*, not only offer substantial insights into the turbulence and melancholy she was experiencing—and the place of Sudan within it—but are also harbingers of what would come to preoccupy her when she became a writer.

Tayeb Salih's *The Wedding of Zein,* a novella in Arabic published in 1962, is heralded as a canonical work of Sudanese literature, due to its ability to capture complex religious, social and individual dynamics in a rural setting.[1] Set in the same village as the one made famous by Salih's *Season of Migration to the North*, it tells the story of a village idiot named Zein, who occupies a peculiarly mystical place within the community. Bizarre-looking, hunched but possessed with brute strength, he is derided and bullied by many. But Zein is also seen as a lucky charm, whereby any girl he falls in love with ends up in a fortuitous marriage. Zein is close with a Sufi saint, Haneen, and other outcasts with disabilities, such as Mousa, Ashmana, and Bakheit, earning him the status of someone with an otherworldly aura and inexplicable powers. "Zein, then, is a unifying force, a harbinger of joy, a messenger of love and a benefactor and it is these many roles that earn him the respect and admiration of Haneen—the holy man."[2]

There is a tendency to view Salih (at least among Western critics) as an irreverent writer who mocked religion; and though he pushed the limits of his characters through satire and explorations of immorality, Salih is a keen observer of the ways in which religious beliefs shape a community. He also shows a particular empathy toward Sufism. It was likely that *The Wedding of Zein* tapped into Leila's melancholic stirrings for an unsullied, pastoral Sudan replete with elements of folklore, while also suitably inspiring her religiosity through the story of an outcast with mystical and spiritual powers. Furthermore, when Leila became a writer a decade later, she was also drawn to characters with disabilities who strained against the strictures of a normative and ableist society.

Salih's world, however, is fundamentally masculine, and Leila's interest in the spaces and psyches of women was reflected in the second book she carried on the bus. The copy that Leila owned of Zeinab Belail's *The Choice*,[3] published with a blood orange cover in 1984, featured a young woman with a lowered gaze and hair askance, cradling her hands in her lap, while a farmer tended to the land in the background. The strange cover belied what a somewhat explicit and "racy" book was.

The female protagonist grows up in a poor but loving home in a small village. A grandmother recounts folktales to the children; the young girl does well in school and at home and seems to have a happy childhood. She eventually falls in love with a young boy, and their romance blossoms when they go off to university in Khartoum. But they are unable to marry due to differences in class. She is eventually married off to another man, but their marriage flounders due to their bad sex life. After spending some years outside of Sudan, the couple returns to Khartoum, where she meets her former lover and starts an affair with him. Suddenly sexually awakened, she also finds herself attracted to her husband, and much to her disdain, begins to sleep with both men. Unable to cope with her own self-loathing and moral failure, she eventually kills herself.

The Choice was an unabashedly feminist novel written in a realist style, and the bold themes were not surprising for Belail. Well-known in Sudan and active within the Sudanese Writers' Union and the Female Writers Association, Belail's literary career spans five novels and several plays, all of which engage with women's issues.[4]

For Leila, *The Choice* not only had the idyllic Sudanese village life and descriptions of Khartoum, especially the university which she missed, but it also had the thread of romance and unrequited love that she went on to develop in her own work. More importantly, the novel was dedicated to a woman's inner life, her desires and pleasures, as well as her fateful moral dilemmas. The novel clearly had an influence on Leila when she began crafting her own intricate women's worlds, exploring questions of love, faith and empowerment within them.

Mona's fellowship in London was coming to an end, and her career in Khartoum was taking off. She was promoted to dean at Cairo University (Khartoum) and had a surge in publications, which meant that Leila would now have to fend for herself going forward. Despite the difficulties, Leila had studied hard and completed the master's. In her mind, there was only one plan: get a PhD, return to Sudan, and have an academic career just like her mother. So off she went to enroll for the MPhil that came before the doctorate.

Baby Kareem had been on a waiting list at the LSE daycare program and finally got in. The daycare itself was a game-changer for Leila, with its progressive policies, beautiful facilities, and the occasional encounter with a fellow parent. The routine had now set itself. With Kareem thriving at the daycare, and the intensity of playing catch-up during the master's program having dissipated, Leila's life should have become infinitely easier. But the heavy, trapped feelings showed no signs of ebbing, and her unhappiness was starting to feel chronic.

The writing was still a long way away, but the three years spent in London were instrumental for Leila with regards to honing the themes, tone and craft in her early works. Her first published story, "Coloured Lights," is an early indicator of the type of work Leila would later produce, especially in the novels *The Translator* and *Minaret.*

"Coloured Lights" begins with a bus commute, fictionalizing the daily ritual where many of her feelings of isolation and melancholy were concentrated, the two Sudanese books clutched for comfort. The story moves back and forth between London and Khartoum, and the first-person narrator entwines the two spaces through flashbacks, as the bus inches its way through crowded London during Christmastime. The narrator is recalling the death of her favorite cousin Taha, who is killed on his wedding day because of an electrical accident involving the colored lights mounted for the festive occasion. The story begins with the narrator admitting she "cried a little as the bus started to fill up," and she wonders if she was "crying for Taha or maybe because I was homesick, not only for my daughters or my family but sick with longing for the heat, the sweat and the water of the Nile."[5]

The grief and isolation of being far away from home find their expression in a tragedy that had occurred a long time ago; the two mournings coalesce into one. "Lights twined around the short trees on the pavements, on wires stretched across the street. Festive December lights. Blue, red, green lights, more elaborate than the crude strings of bulbs that we use in Khartoum to decorate the wedding."[6] Memory blurs the two places into one through the lights, and then again through the London shop windows, where mannequins dressed in finery become a way to recall the green dress worn by the protagonist on Taha's wedding day.

Tina Steiner has argued that "nostalgic memory becomes a lens with which her characters read their new environment in Britain."[7] The memory of Taha's death is stirred up as London's Christmas lights come into view; the memory becomes a channel to indulge in nostalgia for Sudan fused with discomfort with Britain. "I was alienated from this place where darkness descended unnaturally at 4 pm, and people went about their business as if nothing happened." The protagonist admits that perhaps because of the solitude and because her "mind was reeling from the newness" that surrounded her, Taha's memory was suddenly closer to her after many years of his passing.[8]

In "Coloured Lights," the protagonist reflects on the English word "homesick" and finds that an equivalent does not exist in Arabic. The young woman also adds that "[i]t seemed that the fate of our generation is separation, from our country or our family."[9] Homesickness, thus, becomes a potent mirroring device to reflect on one's past and present self, a kind of captivity between two places and two temporalities. In her stories, as in life, homesickness manifests without warning and may be triggered by a kind gesture from a stranger (the West Indian bus driver in the story); or when characters in her novel become objects of Islamophobia and racism in the UK; or even by the simple way in which the light falls; or the flash; or a certain color. These sudden triggers open the narrative space that takes the form of a story or an anecdote from childhood, and are masterfully rendered by Leila with deep sensuality, replete with smells, sounds, colors, and the representation of touch.

Leila's first published story is a powerful and lyrical harbinger of what her fiction will single-mindedly pursue for the first decade of her career. In this world, migration becomes a wound that no balm can cure; leaving home is an irreparable loss, and finding refuge is elusive. Indeed, for Leila, her own move was traumatic. Moreover, her work went on to establish that the price of migrant journeys and challenges of assimilation are often paid by women. Leila developed a writing form that could capture women's complex interiority etched against the backdrop of an Islamophobic Western society.

Sudan lost: Becoming migrant, becoming Muslim

The gnawing alienation and homesickness that Leila felt in London was compounded by her growing knowledge about the macro and microaggressions that Muslims in the West tended to either encounter or observe.

Leila had been convinced from a very young age that she was not particularly political. While current affairs, political analyses, the fate of Sudan, Africa and the world were always part of conversations among her parents, friends and family members, they fell squarely within the realm of the normal socialization of a bourgeois, educated class, who were not always impacted by local or international politics. These were not discussions that arose from a place of passionate and indignant churning, nor were they meant to inspire protest or resistance. Thus, the voyage out of this comfortable and privileged environment to the heart of empire itself meant that Leila was forced to confront a gradually growing angst about what she looked like, sounded like, and presented to the Western world.

It was a London marked by Margaret Thatcher's second decade as Prime Minister, and the questions of immigration, race and racism loomed large in the public sphere. Under Thatcher, a group of journalists, politicians, academics, and others known as the New Right rose to power, and racism became institutionalized in an environment whereby "[m]ulticulturalism and multicultural education were threats because they implied that all cultures were equally valid, valuable and moral, which they were not." The general ideology that racialized people and migrants were responsible for "diluting national, Christian values" was rampant.[10] The "riots from April to July of 1981, which burned in twenty-six cities" certainly haunted the political climate of the time. Anti-Blackness, Islamophobia, and anti-migrant sentiment had firmly taken root.

But Leila was certain that these debates and situations did not apply to her. She was a student from a well-off family, and she would be returning to Sudan as soon as the degree was wrapped up. She was not an immigrant, but rather someone with a short, temporary goal of pursuing higher education. There was no doubt in Leila's mind about an imminent return to Sudan.

Leila's years in London coincided with the controversy around Salman Rushdie's novel, *Satanic Verses,* when a "fatwa" was issued by Ruhollah Khomeini, the Supreme Leader of Iran, that condemned Rushdie to death. Protests by Muslims about the "blasphemous" contents of the book had already broken out in India and in the UK in 1988, and the book was banned in some countries. Framed as a "freedom of speech" concern, it became one of the most contested geopolitical issues of the time, that fabricated, embedded, and sustained a clash between violent, censorious, and barbaric Muslims on one side, and the rational Westerners who valued freedom of speech in art and culture on the other. No matter which way one felt about the book, Muslims living in the West were decidedly at the center of the controversy, and the backlash was enduring. Leila remembers the buzz of the news and the general chatter with family and colleagues at the university. She also began to understand the microaggressions that were part of quotidian interactions, those that insisted (unprovoked) on pedantically explaining how they felt about the book, and why the Muslims were wrong.

Leila's decision to wear a hijab in London was freeing at first, since she was able to avoid criticism over it from her Sudanese circle. But over time, and in this atmosphere, she started to become aware of the fact that her personal choice elicited, at best, a type of objectification, and at worst, aversion. Leila remains reticent about admitting any kind of political consciousness or claiming any affiliations. Yet, it is possible to trace her gradual consciousness around the prejudices toward Africans, Muslims, migrant women, and Islam, more broadly. In the beginning, Leila did not mind explaining where Sudan was; that it was in Africa, that it was next to the much better-known Egypt. But in retrospect, Leila feels that they might have been too tolerant of these racisms that were part and parcel of the overall climate.

Her early fiction portrays this atmosphere but also expresses reticence about the situation. For example, in the short story "The Ostrich," set in London and narrated by Sumra, her student husband Majdy points at graffiti that says,

> Look, "Black Bastards" on the wall of the mosque, "Paki, go home" on the newsagent's door, do you know what it means, do you know who wrote it? I breed a new fear of not knowing, never knowing who these enemies are.[11]

The narrator Sumra can sense the racism, yet she is befuddled and does not wish to investigate it, mirroring the way Leila herself was thinking about the political climate at that time.

The London years might have been unhappy ones, but they were foundational for Leila's overall intellectual, political, and personal growth. She navigated a variety of spaces at this time: the world of the university, the transport system, privileged spaces such as the daycare, and public spaces such as streets, shopping areas, various London parks, and some local mosques. It was through these spaces that her knowledge of self as a woman, a Muslim, a migrant, and an African—and the fundamentally embattled nature of these identities within the UK—began to cohere.

Over time, several of her stories and novels began to engage with these themes in a more deliberate manner. In *The Translator*, published in 1999, a decade after her time in London, when she was living in Aberdeen, Sammar has been assigned to translate interviews being conducted with extremist groups in Egypt. This job opportunity is brought to her by Rae, an academic with expertise in Islam and politics, and thus offers openings in the novel to stage debates on Islam and Islamophobia, the question of terrorism and its associations with Islam, and the production of knowledge about Muslims in the university and in the media. Rae is portrayed as the confident progressive who is critical of Islamophobia and who insists that Muslim extremists are "not the biggest threat facing the Western world. If we look at real terrorist damage, Muslim extremists have caused much less of it than the IRA, the Red Brigade, the Baader-Meinhof gang, the Basque separatist ETA."[12]

Sammar is portrayed as curious but detached, and far more concerned with figuring out Rae and his precise interests and limits regarding Islam rather than political debates. Sammar's main investment is in their relationship. She hopes that Rae's interest and defense of Islam might mean that he will convert to Islam in order to marry her. The dilemmas and conversations in *The Translator*, and the directly political nature of Sammar and Rae's professions, illustrate that Leila's political consciousness is quite well honed by this time, and she is not timid about expressing these present-day strains of racism in the West in her work—though it is rarely done through her women protagonists.

Leila's harshest depiction of Islamophobia and anti-immigrant sentiment occurs in her second novel, *Minaret* (2005). Najwa is harassed by a group of men on the London bus and has a bottle of soda thrown directly at her.

> Laughter from behind me. Something hits the edge of the seat next to me and bounces down the aisle; I don't know what it is. He has missed his target this time. Will they move closer, and what if they run out of things to throw? I look up at the bus driver's face in the mirror. His eyes flicker and he looks away. I stare out of the window but I see my reflection staring back at me. It is best to look down at my shoes. The smooth night traffic means that the bus moves fast. It shouldn't be long now, a couple more stops. I hear footsteps come up behind me, see a blur of denim. He says, "You Muslim scum," then the shock of cool liquid on my head and face. I gasp and taste it, Tizer. He goes back to his friends–they are laughing.[13]

Najwa is targeted because of her hijab, which marks her as a Muslim and an unwanted migrant. Like many of Leila's women protagonists, Najwa does not indulge her anger, nor muse over the politics and policies that have led to the violent event. The trauma is inscribed upon her body as Najwa details her uncomfortable night:

> My chest hurts and I wipe my eyes. The wind hits against my wet scarf, it makes my scalp feel cold. I use the dry edge of the scarf to wipe my face. I breathe in and out to make the anger go away, to let it out through my nose. My cheeks are sticky. I bite my lips and they taste sweet. It could have been beer but I've been lucky. I blink and that's uncomfortable because my eyelashes are twisted and stuck together. I didn't know that eyelashes could ache. I walk the rest of the way home thinking about my eyelashes and that I will have to wash my hair. I don't like washing it at night. My hairdryer doesn't work anymore and I don't sleep well with wet hair. It irritates me, damp and sprawling over the pillow.[14]
>
> (*Minaret*, 80–81)

The description details the impact of the Islamophobic assault on unexpected parts of her body: sticky cheeks, aching eyelashes, wet and uncomfortable hair. While Najwa's journey is compounded by incidents of humiliation and debasement throughout the novel, these are usually attributed to her family, her employers, and her lovers. But the bus incident stands out as the one that offers a critical commentary on being a visibly migrant and Muslim woman in London, and the threat that wearing a hijab poses for her physical being.

Both Sammar and Najwa navigate hostile Western forces, but neither voice their opinions nor express frustration. In her later works, such as *Kindness of Enemies (2015)* and *Bird Summons (2019)*, Leila's protagonists become more vocal and display more agency about social and political issues, but this is a gradual transition. Nonetheless, it is quite clear that there is a definite awareness about her outsider status in the UK, and a defense of Muslims and Islam is intricately woven into her work from the very beginning.

Life in London trudged on, and Nadir's absence in Leila and baby Kareem's life was grating. The sense of separation only felt stronger each time Nadir visited; they all had a wonderful time together, and then inevitably, it was time for him to leave again. Fed up with this push and pull, they decided on an alternate plan where Leila and Kareem decided to join Nadir in Dier oz-Zor, in eastern Syria, in 1989. But things did not quite gel, and neither mother nor baby loved living there. In just a few months, Leila discovered she was pregnant again, and the trio headed back to London. Luckily for everyone, living together in Syria had solidified Nadir's decision to find a job that would keep them all together, and where the times away were not as long.

"It is a nice memory of Nadir looking after Karim at home," Leila recounts, "and me, pregnant, going to Imperial College, getting a big directory, and writing down all the names and addresses of every single oil company in the UK." Leila furnished Nadir with this list, and he sent out his CV and letters. In further improvements, Kareem was back at the same LSE daycare, and Leila was being cared for by a gynecologist within the same system. Though there was no sense of what job Nadir might land and where they would end up, there was optimism in the air and a distinct feeling that life was looking up.

The gray city by the North Sea: Scotland bound

In the summer of 1990, Nadir got a job in Aberdeen and began to commute to London on weekends to see his family. Despite this welcome change, Leila and Nadir's ultimate plan involved them living together. Leila was having an easy pregnancy, and her thesis research and writing were also going smoothly. Mona and Fuad visited at that time, and with Kareem in the care of his efficient grandparents, Leila took a train to Aberdeen to see Nadir and to get a sense of the city. At 34 weeks pregnant, the cool air and small city feeling were refreshing after the muggy London heat. She walked around looking for apartments for the family, as well as nurseries for Kareem. Baby Ahmed arrived in August, and in just two weeks, the family of four was reunited in a one-bedroom apartment in Aberdeen, the northernmost city in Scotland.

The next few months were uneventful, even quiet, with Leila focused on nursing the baby, setting a routine for Kareem, and carrying on with her research and writing. But almost overnight, everything became fraught. Nadir received the news that his mother Judith was diagnosed with melanoma and was to undergo surgery in London. This also coincided with Leila's scheduled meeting with her two advisors at LSE to discuss her future and career. The whole family went down to London for a week.

Judith's surgery went reasonably well, and it would buy her about eight more years of life, though they would be marred by tests and more surgeries.

Leila's meeting with her advisors, however, went terribly awry. She had no real sense of why her supervisors had asked to meet her. In a haze of the newborn baby, and having just moved to a new city, Leila felt she had succeeded in finding a new daily rhythm for her and her children's lives.

Figure 4.1 Leila, Kareem (age 4), and Ahmed (one month old), Aberdeen, September 1990

She was even chipping away at her MPhil thesis with some regularity, so what was to come was a complete shock.

The LSE meeting was convened by her two supervisors, Professor David Bartholomew and Dr. Celia Phillips, and Leila was not particularly close to either of them. The meeting took the form of a take-down. Bartholomew and Phillips told Leila that she had reached the end of the road. Though she was making decent progress on her research, they did not see her advancing to a PhD. They told her that she would receive an MPhil from LSE, but if Leila continued to desire a PhD, she would have to transfer to another university. Leila was so unprepared for this that she did not question their declarations. Humiliated and dismayed, Leila let their words rain down on her.

As she made her way home, several alternate scenarios went through her head. Had she known, she would have firmly declared that she did not agree and asked for time to prove otherwise. Had she known, she would have dazzled them with new research ideas to prove that the MPhil was not the end of the road for her. Had she known, her mother would have prepared her in advance, forced her to exhibit determination and ambition, and to proclaim that she would indeed pursue her PhD. More than anything else, she thought of her mother who would have fought for her and given her direction, determination and audacity. She could hardly wait to get home and speak to Mona.

But another shock awaited Leila. Mona listened to Leila's story but sounded resigned. She told Leila to write up her current research and stop at the MPhil, just as the two professors had advised. Leila could barely believe it. This was a mother whose sole goal had been to ensure that her daughter would earn a doctorate and have a flourishing academic career. Having fought for Leila's success in education every step of the way, it now felt like the ground beneath her feet was rapidly shifting. Mona led, and Leila followed, and this formula had consistently produced the right results since the first days of primary school.

A nagging sense of failure gripped Leila. Every possible self-deprecating thought passed through her mind: that Mona had given up on her; that Leila was not cut out for any kind of career, after all; that Mona had finally realized her daughter wasn't worth fighting for; that Mona had written her off; and that Leila had disappointed her. A sea of negativity engulfed her as she replayed the scenes with the supervisor and then the conversation with her mother. But the most catastrophic realization came much later: Sudan was fading from the horizon.

Leila had cultivated a single-minded view of her future; she would finish her PhD, get a job in Khartoum, Nadir would find something there as well, and they would all live happily ever after in Sudan. But she had been turning a blind eye to political upheavals at home. Bashir seized power in a military coup in 1989, suspended all existing political parties, and was working to institute Islamic law. The coup itself was known to be "bloodless," but plenty of blood flowed soon after with imprisonment, bans, executions, and purges of anything and anyone seen as oppositional. Nadir's parents had already moved out of Sudan, and Mona was back and forth between Egypt and Sudan. Even though Leila's father would stubbornly never leave Sudan come hell or high water, the family felt dispersed and were no longer grounded in Khartoum.

It took a long time for Leila to reorient herself to the idea that her mother was not abandoning her but prioritizing herself instead. Mona had energetically poured herself into setting Leila up in the UK and had helped with the births of both her grandsons. Sudan was changing drastically, and so Mona was strategizing about fully transitioning her own career to Egypt. She was also not getting any younger, and exhaustion had begun to creep in. Despite the plausibility of Mona's shifting priorities, the fiasco at LSE fundamentally altered the mother-daughter relationship. There was no shared goal anymore, and the bond loosened. Mona and Leila found themselves drifting away from each other. Mona began to focus on life in Egypt, and Leila gave in to settling down in Aberdeen.

Gradually, Leila tried to acknowledge the sense of relief that had begun to creep in once it was declared that her academic trajectory had reached a dead end. She felt like she had finally been given some extra time. It would now be easy to nurse the baby, care for Kareem, and finish up her thesis. She could also look at possible PhD programs in Aberdeen at her own pace. She hoped to find her way through this new hand that life had dealt her.

Yet, Leila somehow did not go and explore any PhD programs at universities. She barely even looked them up. Her mind was telling her to fix the PhD problem and get back on track. Her body, however, refused to find itself anywhere near a campus. She gave in to a different routine. She would drop Kareem off at the nursery and bring Ahmed in a pram to the Ferryhill library on Fonthill Road. Built with the gray granite characteristic of the historic buildings in Aberdeen, the Ferryhill library (now closed) was a cozy community space that organized events for children and seniors.[15] Leila would spend some time writing her thesis, but she also started reading voraciously.

A gentle lull set in. The noise from the events at LSE and the bittersweet residue of Mona's abandonment began to fade away. Aberdeen, with its dramatic skies and its pensive gray architecture, suited Leila. The isolation and the grief of her London years were externalized in the poetic gloominess of Aberdeen, allowing her to release the tensions from the pressures of the last few years and the loss of Sudan, her home.

The new rhythm of life was calming, and Leila finished her thesis titled "Stock and flow models for the Sudanese educational system" and submitted it to LSE in the summer of 1991. She flew into London just for the day to defend it. This time around, it seemed that she had walked into a completely different scenario. Her supervisors were complimentary and positive, and invited her to speak about her future later in the day; a future that they were certain she did not have just some months ago.

"I can't, I have to fly back," was Leila's flat response. It indicated just how detached she had become from her work, and the event—that not long ago—had been a big blow. She had perhaps finally admitted to herself that she was not interested in both statistics and academia.

Life in Scotland resumed in earnest. She now gravitated toward the Central Library of Aberdeen, a spacious facility with many great book collections, a vibrant program of events and activities, and large, light-filled reading rooms. She began to read steadily and "seriously." Having had two kids, a mind churning about her relationship with her mother, and feeling a bit adrift in terms of a career, Leila started to suspect that she was experiencing sentiments and dilemmas attributed to women. These were women's problems, and they were being amply represented in all the reading she was coming across. She felt a particular pull toward short stories, and the *Women's Hour Book of Short Stories* anthologies introduced her to a range of writers whom she would come to enjoy reading. She fell in love with the work of Caribbean writer Jean Rhys, and discovered Egyptian writer Ahdaf Soueif, both of whom came to define Leila's sensibility. She read widely, with an open mind, and without an agenda.

The early 90s were a fraught time for Muslims living in the West. The controversy with Salman Rushdie's fatwa was not dying down, and the first Gulf War was underway and very much in the news. Thatcher was not the Prime Minister anymore, but immense damage had been inflicted, and racist, anti-migrant, anti-Black, and anti-Muslim rhetoric had been legitimized. Even so, while Leila and Nadir followed the news, they were in the throes of raising small children, living in a bubble. Nadir was not yet sent to offshore sites, and though he would still leave for short spells, he was generally around and involved. It was their first time living together, stable, as a family, and they began to look for a more permanent home to purchase in Aberdeen.

They were not particularly social at the time either; and when they did socialize, it would be on a trip to London to see Leila's parents. The Aboulelas still owned the flat near Regent's Park, and everyone would convene there from Sudan and the UK. These were happy occasions, where an effervescent Fuad would make plans for dinners and theater. Leila described her father as "grand," and everyone, including Nadir's parents, Judith, and Ahmed, would be swept up in a whirlwind of London fun.

With baby Ahmed now in daycare, Leila started looking for a job. With her MPhil degree in Statistics, both Nadir and she thought it would be easy for Leila to find a number-crunching position, possibly as a data analyst for a company. She applied for some roles but did not get any interviews. On a whim, she called Aberdeen College (now called Northeast Scotland College)[16] and asked if they were looking for someone to teach statistics. She was in luck.

At first, Leila taught a part-time introductory statistics course with classes of about twenty business administration students. Over time, the college began to increase her hours, and she started teaching a few more classes. The teaching itself was easy; the bulk of the work consisted of marking tests. But it was certainly not an intellectually stimulating environment, and even less of a social one. Leila knew that her classes were mandatory, and she was not expecting to be popular, but she was surprised by how unfriendly her colleagues were. Not a single person spoke to her in the shared staff room, and though she imagined that things would change, it began to unsettle her when the icy treatment continued.

In the back of her mind, Leila knew it was racism and xenophobia because she wore a hijab, was a foreigner, and a Muslim. Yet, she was still not used to seeing herself through a lens of marginalization, and there was no public discourse around the type of microaggressions she was observing. "I didn't process it. I was just unhappy." When she did excavate her feelings, it was through her well-honed sense of nostalgia and patriotism. "It was nothing like my life would have been if I was teaching in Khartoum. Nothing," Leila told herself.

Despite this fog hanging over her, Leila and her family were settled in Aberdeen by the end of 1992. They had bought their first house in the drab neighborhood of Portlehen, in the southern outskirts of the city. Lined with one- or two-story homes with small lawns, it exuded a village-like feeling. It was very much a starter house, and after a year spent in a cramped one-bedroom flat, Leila would look back quite fondly at their first proper home. The children were at school, and Leila had found some exercise classes she liked. Sometime around then, a newspaper advertisement for a distance learning course in creative writing caught her eye.

Administered by the National Extension College and priced at two hundred pounds, Leila felt she was being overindulgent; but she needed a hobby, an outlet of sorts. A large sheaf of papers organized in a ring binder arrived for her by mail. The creative writing course, designed by Pat Bryant, started with small writing exercises, such as an account of your day or the weekend, then slowly moved up to writing in different styles, then urged students to write a short story, with the final assignment of writing a novel. A comprehensive, thoughtfully composed, and well-structured course, Leila would preserve the binder over the years and even take it with her when they began to move around again in a few years.

Leila was assigned a tutor, and she was to work at her own pace. When she finished an assignment, she would put it in an envelope and mail it to her tutor. The feedback was always gentle and very positive. "I loved it," she declared. An exciting bonus was the reading lists included in the material. Though Leila was still reading avidly, she was now guided by these lists and would religiously borrow the assigned books from the library.

Leila soon graduated to the short story module. Though she doesn't remember what the story was about, she does recall being pleased with having played around with the narrative style. She showed it to Nadir, who was pleasantly surprised at Leila's talent. Around the same time, an old family friend, Khadija Knight, became an unexpected source of motivation for Leila.

Khadija was a friend of her brother Khalid and was much older, almost her mother's age, but she was from Glasgow and had taken an interest in Leila when the family moved to Scotland. Leila also mailed the story to her, and Khadija told her to find a proper writing class. The University of Aberdeen offered evening classes in creative writing, and buoyed by Khadija's advice, Leila enrolled in one right away.

Something had clicked. The hobby suddenly took over and became a passionate project. She found herself making time away from her daily parenting duties and her teaching job to do something she had never done before: write. Leila had woken up to a new dawn after a long and dark night.

Notes

1 Tayeb Salih, *The Wedding of Zein*, trans. Denys Johnson-Davies (Three Continents Press: 1968).
2 Ali A. Abbas, "Notes on Tayeb Salih: 'Season of Migration to the North' and 'The Wedding of Zein,'" *Sudan Notes and Records*, vol. 55, 46–60.
3 Zeinab Belail with الاختيار *(The Choice)*.
4 "Excerpt from Sudanese Writer Zeinab Belail's Novel 'The Cactus Plant'" in *Sudan Now Magazine*, March 20, 2022, https://sudanow-magazine.net/page.php?subId=30&Id=1437
5 Leila Aboulela, "Coloured Lights," in *Coloured Lights* (Polygon: 2001), 1.
6 Leila Aboulela, "Coloured Lights," in *Coloured Lights* (Polygon: 2001), 3.
7 Tina Steiner (2008) "Strategic nostalgia, Islam and cultural translation in Leila Aboulela's The Translator and Coloured Lights," *Current Writing: Text and Reception in Southern Africa*, vol. 20, no. 2, 7–25.
8 Leila Aboulela, "Coloured Lights," in *Coloured Lights* (Polygon: 2001), 2.
9 Leila Aboulela, "Coloured Lights," in *Coloured Lights* (Polygon: 2001), 3.
10 Jenny Bourne, "'May we bring harmony'? Thatcher's legacy on 'race,'" *Race & Class*, vol. 55, no. 1 (2013), 87–91.
11 Leila Aboulela, "The Ostrich," in *Coloured Lights* (Polygon: 2001), 41.
12 Leila Aboulela, *The Translator* (Heinemann: 2001), 35.
13 Leila Aboulela, *Minaret* (Bloomsbury: 2005), 80.
14 Leila Aboulela, *Minaret* (Bloomsbury: 2005), 80–81.
15 Chris Cromar, "'We're still fighting the fight, we're not going to go away': Anger, sadness and tears as Ferryhill Library closes after 120 years," *The Press and Journal*, March 31, 2023, https://www.pressandjournal.co.uk/fp/news/aberdeen-aberdeenshire/5568949/anger-sadness-tears-ferryhill-library-closes/
16 "North East Scotland College," *Wikipedia*, last edited on September 16, 2025, https://en.wikipedia.org/wiki/North_East_Scotland_College

5 Writing as Refuge

"It was still my secret, my little hobby."

After almost two years of rejections, Leila's debut novel *The Translator* was finally published by a small Scottish press in 1999. The book arrived with very little fanfare—no launches, readings, or celebrations at home—except a sense of satisfaction and accomplishment shared only with Nadir. At this point, very little about her had changed to the outside world. She continued to teach statistics part-time, was a dedicated parent, and remained devoted to her social life with the women at the mosque. The world of writing was only one of Leila's many worlds, and to a degree, it was the one most sequestered from her "real" life.

She was part of a women's writing group in Aberdeen, and the aspiring writers in the group were ambitious, smart, and supportive of each other. In a way, the writing group's trajectories differed significantly as Leila wrote and published with far more frequency and went on to become an established author. Leila's short stories had started appearing in a few reputable local Scottish magazines and journals with some consistency as she slowly found her way in the Scottish literary world. This meant accommodating Sudan with Scotland and Scotland with Sudan, inventing a form that could fuse the ache of homesickness with the sense of home she had slowly begun to find in Aberdeen.

Eventually, "The Museum," her story of a young Sudanese student who finds herself amongst African artifacts on a museum date with a Scottish man, won the first-ever Caine Prize for African Writing in 2000. Soon after, *The Translator*, which similarly told the love story of Sudanese Sammar and older Scottish man Rae, was longlisted for the Orange Prize for Women's Fiction, one of the UK's more prestigious awards.

Writing soon went from a hobby for working through exile to soaring professional success.

***

DOI: 10.4324/9781003306719-6

A writer blossoms

In late 1992, Leila's creative writing course met in the evenings at the University of Aberdeen. Nadir was home with their two boys, Kareem and Ahmed, as Leila joyfully took her first steps into a whole new world. Almost without warning, a path had opened to her and split her life into two: the before and the after of becoming a writer. The "before" was tinted with nostalgia; Sudan became a place she inhabited intimately in her writing. And the "after" ushered in a completely new Leila, strident, focused, and ambitious. Now, it was as if she was seeing differently and the world around her was laid out in vivid color. She was filled with ideas and observations, and every free moment was spent making notes, typing stories, and reading books that were either recommended to her by the instructor or her creative writing friends.

The course was Leila's first real taste of a professional writing class; her peers were serious, and the class was more advanced than the distance learning course. It was a diverse group in terms of race and nationalities, and the British male instructor created a workshop atmosphere. Students read each other's work and offered feedback. Although some writers received harsh commentary, Leila did not. She remembers the feedback to have been positive and encouraging. After having spent so many years struggling and persevering through multiple statistics degrees with critical professors and an overbearing mother, it was a liberating feeling for Leila to love something so easily and succeed at it so effortlessly. The imposter feeling she carried with such weight may not have disappeared, but it was certainly becoming more distant.

In the class, Leila struck up a friendship with an American woman of the same age, Priscilla Frake. In a way, Leila and Priscilla were leading mirroring lives. Priscilla's husband was working in the oil industry too, though unlike Nadir, he was working for Chevron and had a hefty "expat package" with a big house and generous perks. Priscilla had studied to be a petroleum engineer but was an aspiring poet, with ambition and knowledge of writing as a vocation. In the shadow of Priscilla's ambition and self-assuredness, Leila slowly found her own amateur approach to writing dissipating. Priscilla lent her the *Poets and Writers* magazine and books like Amy Tan's *The Joy Luck Club* and Natalie Goldberg's *Writing Down the Bones.* She also told Leila about prestigious creative writing programs in the US and schooled her in that infamous process called the "publishing track."

Leila's first submission for the class was the short story titled "Visitors." Amina, a young doctor, works at an outpatient clinic in Khartoum and takes a fancy to Hassan, a rather beautiful little boy with polio. After he is discharged from the clinic, Amina drives the family home to the mud shack in a poor neighborhood on the outskirts of the city. They invite her in, but she promises that she will visit the week after. Pleased with herself, Amina shows up as promised, laden with gifts. Hassan's mother, Zeinab, rushes to be hospitable, and soon the neighborhood folk gather to see the important and ostensibly wealthy visitor. Amina enjoys the attention and educates them on various health matters, even writing up prescriptions. Zeinab says she will return the visit, and Amina is surprised. When the family does show up at her home in the best clothing and shoes they can muster, Amina is irritable. She feels self-righteous anger well up as she decides that the family has shown up to beg and take advantage of her. But the tables are turned as Zeinab gifts Amina the most precious commodity in Sudan, one that is being severely rationed: white sugar.

Leila's classmates praised the story and especially appreciated her descriptions of Sudan and the way she developed the characters. In a way, many of Leila's archetypal themes can be found in "Visitors." She alternates between the flow of Amina's inner thoughts and vivid descriptions of the setting, revealing her gift for constructing a specifically female interiority and an ability to create an intimate sense of place, capturing the small details of an interaction between characters from different class settings and the inherent disconnection and misunderstanding embedded within such a setup. And finally, there is a moral element as the young, self-assured, middle-class woman is taught a lesson in humility, having to confront her own vanity and the limits of her generosity.

Validated by her instructor and her peers in the writing class, and armed with a few complete stories, some knowledge about the publishing industry, and a rising ambition to be a proper writer, Leila, along with Priscilla, stumbled upon an interesting opportunity available at Aberdeen's Central Library. The local newspaper had carried news about Todd McEwen, who would be a writer-in-residence at the library for the 1993–1994 academic year. He would be available by appointment to read and comment on any creative work presented to him. Leila and Priscilla jumped at the opportunity and gathered their materials together.

Todd was an American from California of proud Scottish heritage, who had started living and working in Scotland as a young man. With many publications under his belt and married to the successful Scottish writer Lucy Ellman, he was well connected in the American and British publishing industries. He worked on and off at *Granta* magazine in the eighties and completed residencies and teaching gigs in the UK. He read three of Leila's polished stories, "Coloured Lights," "The Ostrich," and "Tuesday Lunch."

He invited Leila and Priscilla into a small class of ten students that he had handpicked during his first few months at the library. Classes were held at the library and at the Lemon Tree Arts Center. Todd inaugurated the class with Leila's story "Tuesday Lunch," which narrated a vignette from a school day in the life of eight-year-old Nadia, who is under strict instructions from her mother not to eat pork. But little Nadia is unable to ask the teacher for the chicken meal and eats the pork after all. She spends the next day and night in great turmoil about having betrayed her mother.

Todd was clearly impressed with Leila's talent and went out of his way to help her get published and to learn the ropes of the industry. For Leila, Todd's class was an eye-opening experience. For her, Todd's theory that "writing was an extension of reading" became a touchstone. The world of writing became incredibly exciting, and because of Todd's commitment to centering Scottish work, the literary universe also felt accessible and within reach. He made the class read the winners of important Scottish literary prizes and works about Scottish identity, such as Jeff Torrington's anti-Thatcher novel *Swing Hammer Swing!*, which made an impression on Leila. Thirty years later, Leila remembers that when she "went to writing workshops, everyone spoke about the latest Scottish novels. We were enthusiastic about Janice Galloway, Irvine Welsh, and A.L. Kennedy. It was an exciting time for Scottish literature—and I was inspired and encouraged by the mood around me."[1]

But these works were read simultaneously with Black, African and postcolonial writers like Abdulrazak Gurnah, Caryl Phillips, Anita Desai, and Jean Rhys. Such writers were not yet in the mainstream imagination but had become part of Leila's world because of her mother-in-law Judith, the lists from the distance-learning course, and from the sporadic displays at Aberdeen libraries. Leila confessed that the writers who moved to the UK "in their youth struck a special chord with me as outsiders grappling with issues similar to my own."[2] Her understanding of Scotland and Scottish identity was deepening, but it was always filtered through the perspective of a Muslim, migrant, Sudanese and African living there. In her writing, she attempted to express the sense of disconnect between the two cultures while also striving to belong. This particular and highly unique Sudanese-Scottish hybrid went on to become Leila's signature style.

Todd's choice of the Lemon Tree Arts Center as a location was also pivotal, and Leila was exposed to a steady flow of plays and performances, in addition to the writers that Todd invited for readings and book launches. Priscilla initiated a women's writing group and hosted an inaugural meeting that included the women writers from Todd's class. The writers exchanged their work and offered commentary, but they also discussed ways of getting published. It was a stimulating time for Leila; she would be brimming with ideas, pouring herself into writing whenever she found the time. The alienating world of statistics classes fell away, and the low din of homesickness and longing for Sudan was finding expression in fiction.

Aberdeen as home

Aberdeen was becoming home. Not only had she begun frequenting literary and cultural spaces, but she had also started to visit her local mosque and found herself in a community of Muslim women. The Aberdeen Mosque and Islamic Center on Spital Road was a modest structure located on the high part of a sloping, picturesque cobblestone road that wound down into the University of Aberdeen campus. The family of four had moved from Portlethen and acquired a new four-bedroom house in Ferryhill, in the center of town, within walking distance of Duthie Park along the banks of the River Dee. The mosque was very close, as was the college where Leila continued teaching statistics part-time.

The mosque group consisted of many young women, mothers in particular, who were also from somewhere else: Algeria, Morocco, Lebanon, Iraq, South Asia, and the Gulf. Occasionally, Sudanese families would also pass through. The women spent most of their time in the basement allocated to them and found refuge from an outside world in which they still sought to find a footing.

Leila found herself happily swept up in planning dinner parties, baby showers and birthdays, as well as the occasional meal train if a family was coping with illness or hospitalization. She would often drive people who had not finished their paperwork to obtain their various permits. To the mosque women, she was a beloved mother hen, but she was also a professor with good English, often tasked with helping new arrivals with writing CVs and filling out job applications.

This easy, warm camaraderie and the feeling of refuge is captured in *Minaret,* which Leila admits was inspired by her Aberdeen mosque group, even though the novel was set in London. The mosque setting is also featured in *Bird Summons* and in some of the stories set in Aberdeen. In a short story written in first person titled "Barbie in the Mosque," Leila captures the diversity, intimacy, and inclusiveness of the mosque space as the women wait languidly for the evening prayers with the "tinkling blur" of various languages around them. The protagonist, Leila herself, fiddles with one of the children's toys, a Barbie doll, while chatting with Aisha, a white woman who has converted to Islam. Despite the differences in their backgrounds, their unlikely bond is possible due to the sealed-off safety of the mosque. Leila ruminates: "Outside is a city that knows nothing about us. Outside is a Europe uneasy with our presence. Outside they speak in a different way."[3] Even though the mosque and the women's worlds within it are explored in her fiction, it is also in Leila's real life that this social world becomes particularly important and finally breaks the sense of estrangement that had been weighing on her since moving to the UK.

By the mid-90s, Leila's life was indeed radically different from the plodding years that had preceded it. But these happier worlds that she inhabited were also separate from one another. There was the vibrant intellectual and creative life with the classes and events; the women's writing groups and workshops; there was the other women's group in the mosque who did not really know about Leila's creative writing pursuits; and there was also Leila's extensive family network in Sudan and Egypt with whom she stayed in regular and dedicated contact.

These were difficult political years in Sudan, and there was a lot of flux as family and friends left the country and settled elsewhere. Nadir's parents had already left Sudan, and the nineties were marked by his mother Judith's battle with cancer. In 1993, Bashir nationalized Cairo University's Khartoum Branch where Mona was employed. The Egyptian staff was deported, and Mona now moved her career to Cairo. However, her husband Fuad refused to leave Khartoum. The world had always been Mona and Fuad's oyster, and they both were exceptionally mobile. Their individual ambitions always complemented each other, and they had not only set their two children on favorable life paths but had also stayed deeply tied to the larger family in Sudan and Egypt. But the impasse had finally arrived, and Mona's lifelong dedication to Sudan was finally spent.

Her older brother was in Cairo, and her son, Khalid, had married an Egyptian woman, Rania, and was living and working in Cairo as well. Mona's career was only "going up, up, up," as she recalled, and by 1995, publications and consultation offers were flowing. She had also become the head of the Department of Demography and Vital Statistics at Cairo University in Cairo. Fuad chose Sudan, despite the daily violence and upheavals that came with Bashir's regime. Always the epitome of a couple that was surprisingly compatible despite their intense individualism, they managed to perfect a model of being apart together even in their older age. They established a long-distance routine, with Fuad doing the bulk of the traveling to Cairo. Mona and Fuad would then travel together to London and Aberdeen to see Leila and her young family.

Swept up in these new arrangements steered by Mona, and that mandated Cairo as the new center for family reunions, Leila stayed away from Sudan. A staggering 13 years passed before she returned home.

Leila was engrossed in her Aberdeen life and shoved all the bad news from Sudan under the rug, ingesting only the flux that the rest of her family seemed to be experiencing, but from a distance. Bashir's horrific violence toward women, and the systematic destruction of the functioning sectors of Sudanese society did not have a totalizing impact on Leila and her family. Yet she could not even bring herself to engage with the news and negativity—even from a cold, distant perspective. There was a mulish obstinacy in her love and patriotism, and she explained that for her "Sudan is something essential." Despite knowing of the turbulence, Leila insisted to herself that "the Nile is still there. The house is still there. My dad is still there." She was shielded by her Aberdeen bubble, her two boys, her newfound love of writing, and her exciting social life. In Leila's mind, she was not writing about Sudan's turmoil. Yet, much of the anxiety about a declining Sudan is reflected in the early stories through quick flashes, as migrant protagonists hear news from home, usually through phone calls.

Todd's mentorship helped Leila and Priscilla to better understand the literary culture of the moment, and both realized that their path to publishing started in Scotland. The nineties were a time of transformation for Scotland, and the industrial decline of the Thatcher era had impacted the region tremendously. Resistance was in the air, but so was revival. The economy was getting better, and pride in Scottish culture and history was growing. In 1990, Glasgow was declared the European City of Culture and became a pioneering and "powerful example of culture-led regeneration for cities."[4] Shaking off its reputation as a city of poverty, violence, and crime, Glasgow made efforts to develop tourism through literary festivals, films, and concerts. A new theater and arts scene also began to thrive.

These were Leila's most energetic years, and her own drive and ambition to become a published author likely surprised her as well. She would mail out photocopies of her most workshopped short stories along with cover letters to various magazines and literary journals every day. Leila's first story was published in *Mica*, a student-run literary magazine at the University of Aberdeen in their summer 1993 issue. It was her most polished draft of "The Visitors." The issue also carried three poems by Priscilla. Over the next three years, a number of anthologies and magazines included work by Leila and Priscilla in the same volume.

Leila's professional debut came two years later. Her story "Coloured Lights" was published in November 1995, in the 82nd issue of *Chapman*, a literary magazine that prided itself on publishing the "best Scottish writing."[5] Chapman was founded in 1970 when "there was almost no interest in Scottish writing in the UK, Europe and the world at large—and most conspicuously in Scotland." Their "bold and interventionist" journey was defined by the struggle to carve out a space for new and old writers, against a backdrop of derision, neglect, and disrespect for Scottish writing.[6] Their project was political and pedagogical at the core. "Coloured Lights" was included in an issue dedicated to Hamish Henderson, a communist poet and intellectual known as the "founding father of Scotland's 20th-century folk renaissance."[7] Even though the story's setting alternated between London and Khartoum, her residence in Aberdeen, and her immersion in the city's small literary scene allowed her to claim space in this magazine.

Scottish revival and cultural pride permeated Leila's literary circles. Eddie Gibbons, a poet from Todd's group, assembled a volume called *Left to Write: An Anthology of Prose and Poetry by the Lemon*

Tree Writers, which was funded by the Aberdeen City Council. Eddie described it as a "truly international anthology" that included writers and poets from all over the world. The anthology had an ethos of ambition and declared an interest in breaking new ground. Todd's blurb for the book declared that "topics and forms in this book reflect, at last, the polyglot town that Aberdeen has become; the north-east of Scotland inextricably part of the big dirty world."[8] Leila's short, two-page story "Desert Stars," her only story set in Deir el Zor, Syria, was placed first in the book, and poems by Priscilla Frake followed a few pages in.

One year later, Scottish writer Yvonne Spence published an anthology titled *Special Reserve: New Writing from Women in Aberdeen* with the Scottish Cultural Press. Yvonne had been in Leila's creative writing class at the university and, according to Leila, "she was ahead of her time in her support for women's writing, her sensitive awareness of the misogyny in some leading Scottish texts and her understanding of how the Scottish literary scene of the time was heavily dominated by men." Leila admired her fierceness and recalled that Yvonne had walked out of an Irvine Welsh event in Aberdeen because of the sexist extract he had chosen to read.

Yvonne clearly valued Leila and was not only sensitive to the representation gap with women's writing but also understood that diversity was missing in the Scottish scene. *Special Reserve* carried not one but two stories from Leila, a few poems by Priscilla, as well as works by some of the other participants in the women's writing group. Leila's provocative story "Tuesday Lunch," told from the perspective of eight-year-old Nadia, debuted in Yvonne's anthology, as did "Teargas," which was revised and published as "Missing Out" in Granta magazine almost 15 years later.[9]

The debut novel

It would soon be ten years since Leila moved to the UK, and her life had transformed fundamentally. Leila was a new person: confident, ambitious, and in charge of her own destiny. The feeling of failure and humiliation about not being invited to pursue a PhD in Statistics at the London School of Economics (LSE) was lodged in the back of her mind and tended to erupt in her writing whenever her women protagonists grappled with the weight of expectations from families and society.

The distance from her mother, Mona, had allowed Leila to discover herself anew, armed with an exceptional and almost miraculous gift: the ability to express herself through storytelling. Buried under the timid image that Leila projected to the world was a person who was intellectually and creatively activated by social interactions, and who had sharp observations about people, politics, religion, identity, and gender. Though she never exhibited activist tendencies, she bristled with a quiet anger and wrote in defense of migrant Muslim women.

Launched as a writer, Leila's short stories appeared routinely in Scottish publications, and she was invited to contribute to Scottish collections and anthologies. Daily life was hectic but happy. She continued to teach statistics, attend workshops and gatherings with the women writers, and remained immersed in the women's group at the mosque. Though she was not someone who could be perceived as attention-seeking, she was coming to enjoy being praised for her stories in writing class and being needed by the women at the mosque. Her desire to write and all the excitement and freedom that it provided was her *raison d'être*. She found herself hurtling headlong into a novel.

Though she was not a newcomer to a foreign country anymore, Leila still felt a residual homesickness and alienation, the sense of not being understood or accepted, and her nostalgia for Sudan remained. The impossibility of connection between two cultures, two religions, and two races was foremost in her mind. This first novel was aspirational; an attempt to bridge the distance between these worlds. But it was also about seeking autonomy and self-fulfillment, specifically as a Muslim woman who was navigating her faith and her practice of Islam in a fundamentally Islamophobic, Western world. However, beneath the surface of these heavy themes were two of Leila's older preoccupations: romance and marriage.

In terms of style, mood, themes and characters, *The Translator* conjures up a new world that stands distinct from the handful of short stories Leila had been producing. *The Translator* is the story of Sammar, a young Sudanese widow consumed by the grief of her husband's death four years ago. After that, she sent her young son back to Khartoum to be cared for by her mother-in-law, and she leads a small, austere, and isolated life in Aberdeen. Sammar's isolation is shattered as she finds herself drawn into the world of Rae, an older Scottish man who is a professor at the university and has commissioned Sammar for a translation job.

The narrative perspective of *The Translator* is in third person but completely contained within the world of the diminutive and melancholic Sammar. When we first meet Sammar, her period of mourning was long past, but self-neglect and self-loathing had become second nature to her. "Grief had formed, taken shape, a diamond shape, its four angles stapled onto her forehead, each shoulder, the top of her stomach."[10] Grief for Sammar has become such an all-encompassing malady that she even refers to her small, stripped-down room as a hospital: "Four years ill in a hospital she had made for herself. Ill, diseased with passivity, time in which she sat doing nothing."[11]

Sammar's perspective is anchored through her body. The reader grasps her acute self-consciousness and feelings of insecurity as they manifest through aches and discomforts. For her, "light was a source of suffering.

And a headache, pain greater than childbirth." She often finds that worlds are colliding and blending, creating hallucinatory sensations. Early in the novel, Sammar feels as if she had "climbed the stairs into a hallucination which the world had swung around."[12] The fog in Aberdeen often merges with a sense of fogginess in her head. At one point, she confesses that for years, it was "as if there were a fog blocking her vision, a dreamy heaviness everywhere."[13] She is listless, unhappy, and captive to her past, all of which is expressed through headaches, body aches, hallucinations, and feeling foggy. Her faith keeps her going from day to day, yet the overall picture is extremely bleak.

Many of the themes and formal aspects of *The Translator* return in Leila's later works. The high level of awareness about her body and a hyper-attention to her own moods serve to build out the complex interior life of a lonely Muslim woman. Sammar's interiority is a distinctive confluence of psychological and religious consciousness. This way of composing female interiority generates a push-and-pull dynamic in the protagonist's sense of empowerment and agency. Even as Sammar is presented as a submissive and timid person to the outside world, the reader becomes intimate with the contrasting, action-inspiring strength that she draws from her religion, prayer, and reading the Quran. As readers inhabit her inner world, they see how faith equips her with a strong spine, grounds her, and provides her with keen self-awareness, even as she struggles with decisions and events. This style of narration was to become Leila's signature in later novels, especially *Minaret* and *Bird Summons.*

The Translator also reveals Leila's early preoccupation with mental health and questions of disability under the larger umbrella of misfit characters and bodies. Her short story, "The Ostrich," was about the ways in which the protagonist Sumra projects her self-consciousness and unease about being a migrant woman upon a man disfigured in a car accident. With Sammar in *The Translator*, this unease is developed in detail. Sammar experiences a debilitating type of grief; she does not eat for four days and gets headaches where any light feels blinding. Words like "blurry" and "foggy" describe the weather and her mood. Sammar is fatigued easily, constantly feels disconnected from people, and shows all signs of a lingering depression. Even though the novel never names it as such, Leila is deeply invested in depicting a truthful version of Sammar's mental health.

Factors such as alienation from her surroundings, her feeling of not being understood as a foreigner, and the overarching atmosphere of hostility in the UK toward Muslims contribute to a troubled sense of self, weakening Sammar's confidence once the husband whom she relied on is no more. Leila's intimate look at a migrant Muslim woman's consciousness and mental health is developed in future novels as well: through the character of Najwa in *Minaret*, women in many of the short stories, and the three protagonists of *Bird Summons.* Physical disability is also explored at length in *Lyrics Alley,* with the quadriplegic protagonist Nur, and then again in *Bird Summons* through the young boy Adam, who has severe cerebral palsy.

Another notable aspect of *The Translator* is its political thrust. Certain characters are deployed to combat Islamophobia, and several of the scenes depict political and theological debates on Islam. Rae, a scholar and professor of Middle Eastern studies, is a vocal critic of Western policies and racist attitudes toward Muslims. Leila introduces Rae as someone who "knew the Sahara" and had "written a book called *The Illusion of an Islamic Threat.*"[14] Rae was a renowned "expert" on Islam and was invited by the media to speak about politics in Muslim countries. He repeatedly offers historical nuance and clear-eyed analysis of politics in Muslim countries. Rae also attempts to de-link terrorism from Islam by insisting that there are plenty of other examples of terrorism from organizations that are not Muslim at all. Through Sammar's perspective, the reader is given a biography of Rae, and how he lived in Morocco and traveled to various places in the Middle East, attempted to become a journalist, and eventually found his calling in teaching and research. It is important for Leila to frame Rae as a legitimate thinker whose views will be taken seriously in an Islamophobic West; someone who is thoughtful, logical, and analytical rather than a radical lefty with a knee-jerk critique of Western government.

Sammar's colleague and friend Yasmin also offers opinions about Islam in politics and culture. Yasmin is of Pakistani origin, and a practicing Muslim who speaks confidently about the news, the perception of Muslims in the West, and most importantly for Sammar, she is able to offer information and insights into Rae, whom she works for. Both Yasmin and Rae are set up as mirrors for the less opinionated and shy Sammar, whose personality and upbringing have meant that she has neither the confidence nor the vocabulary to engage in intellectual or political reflections.

Yet for Leila, it is important to depict Sammar's deep-seated faith and her difficult migration experience in Aberdeen through an intellectual and political lens. Rae stands in to inform the reader about the political moment that Scotland and the West broadly find themselves in, and Yasmin externalizes Sammar's doubts and fears about romance with Rae, religious conversion, and interfaith marriage. This method of structuring a defense of Islam in *The Translator* replicates in many of Leila's stories and novels, especially in *Minaret, Kindness of Enemies,* and *Bird Summons.*

The Translator emerged out of a "tension" between cultures:

> I am fascinated by cultures coming together. I myself grew up with parents of different nationalities—even though arguably Egypt and Sudan are neighbours and share many similarities. However, growing up with this mixed heritage was a source of tension. Which accent

> should I speak: Egyptian or Sudanese? Should I dress Egyptian like my mother or wear the Sudanese national dress like my cousins and aunts? And on what basis should I decide? Personal feelings, peer pressure, or acquiesce to the more dominant culture? Having lived through these perplexities, I was attuned, once I arrived in Britain, to pick up the intercultural dilemmas between Muslims and the West.[15]

In a way, Leila unknowingly attracted these dynamics to herself. She fell in love with Nadir, whose half-Sudanese and half-British background exposed her to yet another intercultural marriage in which the British woman Judith converted to Islam and embraced Sudanese culture wholeheartedly. Something of Judith surely slipped into the way Rae's character was developed, even though it was much more common for a woman to convert to her husband's religion and culture than the other way round. Leila had a fine-tuned capacity to observe clashes and tensions between cultures, and she found a way to tell stories that explored these dilemmas by resisting the narratives circulated by the dominant culture.

The Translator is divided into two parts: the first set in Aberdeen, and the second in Khartoum. Leila used a quotation from Tayeb Salih's *Season of Migration to the North* as an epigraph to Part 2. When the novel's unnamed narrator returns from England to his village in Sudan, upon finding himself in his familiar childhood home, the narrator declares that "the fog cleared…and I experienced a feeling of assurance." Through the epigraph, Leila announces to the reader that Sammar experiences relief and clarity upon her return home in Khartoum; and home here is also the city and the nation where she can re-belong without question.

Salih's novel was an important touchstone for Leila, and while the two works had many themes in common, the unabashed woman's perspective of *The Translator* could not be more different from Salih's masculinist narrative. Leila also did not engage in any of the thrilling sex and violence elements that are so integral to Salih's novel. For the Anglophone literary world, the English translation of *Season of Migration to the North* was often the most popular, easily available, and oft-taught work of literature from Sudan. In a way, Leila's *The Translator* updated the literary narrative about Sudan, Sudanese characters, and a contemporary migration story, and thus comparisons between the two were inevitable.

Twenty-five years later, it is not clear how and when exactly Leila wrote *The Translator*. "I was trying to write whenever I could," she says. "I was all over the place and there was no routine." Nadir was gone for six-week stretches at this point, and Leila was busy with the children and their school. And there was a lot of social activity with the women's group at the mosque with a flurry of dinners, get-togethers, and baby showers. Yet it was clear that Leila kept her focus and recruited her trusted advisors to read chapters of the novel. Priscilla read early chapters of the novel, but she was also on her way back to the US. Todd was the most encouraging and helped Leila polish the first three chapters of the book as one long story. He sent it to a contact at *The New Yorker*, but they showed no interest in it.

Leila soldiered on with the working title "Translating," which Todd asked her to change to "The Translator" once he read the complete draft. Leila's most steady, committed, and supportive reader was her husband Nadir, a role that continues to this day. He speaks of remaining amazed at his wife's talent and ability to draw detailed descriptions of places and people. Leila shared her novel with Nadir in installments and took a lot of his feedback seriously.

The Translator was written in fits and starts, and during one interruption, she wrote the short story "The Museum," which unexpectedly would be the breakthrough that catapulted her to success.

"The Museum" was a microcosm of *The Translator;* the same elements of inter-racial and intercultural romance, cultural collusion, and female migrant interiority shaped by hyper awareness of the body ran through the story. Protagonist Shadia is a new arrival in Aberdeen enrolled for an MSc in Statistics. Lacking the background required for the coursework, Shadia feels "like someone tossed around by monstrous waves," and her eyes "bulged with fright, watered from the cold."[16] Having left behind a vibrant social life, a large family of five sisters, and her fiancé Fareed, Shadia spends her weekends remembering life in Khartoum and making long-distance calls. Stressed and distracted, she finds herself fascinated with a classmate named Bryan. Even though his blond ponytail and earring were alien to her and symbolized "the strangeness of the West, another culture shock."[17] Bryan, much like Rae, is superior to Shadia because of his mastery of the subject and good grades. Shadia might want to request his notes, but the reader can tell that she also covets his attention.

The story depicts international students from the "Third World": Ethiopia, Malaysia, Nigeria, Turkey, and Sudan. The international students are at a disadvantage because they are new to the Scottish university system and are encumbered by the racism and xenophobia they experience in the city. Accounts range from the Malaysian student whose windows are smashed by "racists," to feeling slighted when the white students like Bryan never sit with the international group in the cafeteria.

Shadia, like Sammar, attempts to bridge the distance between the two groups. She walks over to Bryan and asks for his notes, convinced the whole time that he's grubby, ill-mannered, and badly dressed. She tells herself that his heavy Scottish accent means that her English is better than his. When he hands over his notes in two folders, she is so overwhelmed by his immaculate handwriting and organization that she starts weeping, staining a page from his notes with her tears.

The metaphor of the fog returns in "The Museum" as Shadia feels the "fog lifting" due to the clarity of Bryan's beautifully written notes. As she engages with his notes, she is drawn to him and finds the confidence to chat with him. When he asks her on a coffee date, she dismisses him by telling him she doesn't like his earring or his hair. Bryan is unfazed and asks her out again, sans earring and with a trim, new haircut. Eventually, Shadia agrees to go with Bryan to a museum, which has an exhibit on Africa.

The exhibit glorifies colonial conquest and applauds Scotland's role in empire-building. The statues, placards, and images become a source of stress for Shadia, who had hoped to see beautiful photographs of Africa that would allow her to take a trip down memory lane. As attraction between the two characters surges, the weight of the cultural, linguistic, and social differences becomes unbearable for Shadia. Sammar in *The Translator* asserts her need for Rae to convert to Islam and meet her halfway, but in "The Museum," Shadia decides that she is unable to make the effort. "He didn't know it was a steep path she had no strength for." The setting of the museum, the misrepresentation of Africa and its people, and the cumulative sense of insult and humiliation that it heaps upon Shadia become too much to bear. The story concludes with Shadia telling herself that she would have made an effort to teach Bryan a new language and to explain her culture "[i]f she was not small in the museum."[18]

The nineties were a time of much activity in Leila's personal life with her busy family and her writing and being published. Thanks to Priscilla, Leila had become a fan of *Wasafiri*, a British magazine that featured a diverse roster of international authors. She had submitted work to them, some of which had gotten published. A chance encounter with a Lebanese woman at her mosque opened yet another pathway: gigs writing radio plays for the BBC. The woman had handed her an open call seeking ethnic writers, and Leila submitted "Tuesday Lunch." This led to an interview in Glasgow with a British Indian woman, Shefali Malhotra, who had been tasked with finding new writers and new materials for BBC's radio programs. BBC Radio 4 and BBC World Service commissioned Leila to turn her stories into radio plays. She stepped outside of her comfort zone and started reworking her stories, which not only meant steady paychecks, but also opened up a new network of literary connections. Her radio run started with the story "Visitors," and over the years, she continued to produce some two dozen radio plays, a majority of which have never been published in print form.

Stephanie Cabot from the London talent agency William Morris asked to be Leila's literary agent based on a recommendation from the BBC producer. It was a time of "breakthroughs," as Leila described it, and she happily agreed to let Stephanie represent her. Leila now had an agent who loved the manuscript of *The Translator*.

But *The Translator* continued to receive rejections; the most surprising one was from the Heinemann African Writers Series, given their long record of publishing debut authors from all over Africa. Heinemann, however, remained interested in Leila, and asked for two of her stories for an anthology of women's writing. Leila sent "The Museum" and "Majed" to the editor, the prolific Zimbabwean writer Yvonne Vera. Vera assembled one of the first anthologies of writing by African women, *Opening Spaces*, and included "The Museum."[19]

The rejection by the African Writers series prompted Leila to think carefully about how to position herself as a writer: should she publish as an African writer or as a Scottish writer? Thus far, the Scottish literary scene had been receptive to Leila's writing, and it had seemed like the appropriate route to pursue. Her instinct was right, and eventually, a small University of Edinburgh imprint called Polygon accepted the manuscript for publication. The publication timeline felt slow, but *The Translator* was on its way to seeing the light of day.

Finally, in September 1999, *The Translator* was published. Leila had just turned 35, and this was a momentous occasion, but she admitted that "there was no celebration and I was nervous." Leila's imposter syndrome was back with a vengeance as her novel now joined the literary stacks in bookstores, and review copies went out to newspapers and journals. Unlike the heavy promotional mechanisms deployed today, only famous writers got book launches and book tours back then. Even at home, there was no fuss at all: "I didn't speak about it to my children or my parents. Only Nadir was aware." Writing was still like her secret hobby, one that had not yet translated into a career.

The novel might not have had a dazzling debut, but it had certainly landed. The reception was uneven. There was a desire to valorize Scotland's diversity on the one hand, but also an incapacity to embrace the different worlds and viewpoints that such diversity opened up. *The Translator* was one of the first novels by a "minority" writer to be published in Scotland, and local reception of the work tended to reveal that. In *The Scotsman*, writer Sharon Norris included *The Translator* in her double book review, which led with the diversity of new Scottish writing. But she had very little praise for Leila's book and panned it in unkind terms. While acknowledging the series of juxtapositions and contrasts that Leila straddles in the book, Norris declares that it is a "bad Barbara Cartland," with an unconvincing central love story. The reviewer's hesitant praise involved calling it "an articulate apologia for Islam" and "an interesting social critique." To the reviewer's credit, the second debut novel being reviewed, *Small Town Antichrist* by Iain Grant, is not spared either. Norris deemed it "odd" and "limited."[20]

The acerbic, Scottish critique was drowned out by a small but elegant review that appeared in the far more important *The Guardian* on the same day. *The Translator* was included in the paperbacks section of the Saturday Review, with three other works of fiction and two works of non-fiction, all reviewed by Carris O'Grady. The short burst of praise captured the essence of the novel's nostalgic tone, and calling it a "gentle and melancholy novel," O'Grady found Leila "a wonderfully poetic writer" and wrote that it was "a pleasure to read a novel so full of feeling and yet so serene."[21] Once the big metropolitan newspaper set the tone, the local newspapers had to reckon with Leila's debut novel.

Within two months, Aberdeen's *The Press and Journal* followed up with a half-page spread that carried an author profile, along with a pensive and smiling photo of Leila holding a copy of *The Translator*. Titled "Bridging the Culture Gap," writer Susan Mansfield led with O'Grady's praise from the "London-based" paper. The generous profile offers a quick biographical sketch of Leila from her upbringing in Sudan to the move to Scotland and connects the themes of *The Translator* to Leila's life and preoccupations. There is a focus on Leila's "fascination" with the "interplay of cultures," and she is cast as a "translator" who is "translating her culture, her faith, for those in the country in which she now lives."

Mansfield also includes Leila's observations on Aberdeen as a small but warm and friendly city, one that she much prefers over the cosmopolitan cities like London, where people tended to remain in their own cliques. The profile presents Leila as keen to be accepted and embraced by Scotland, and steers away from anything that might resemble discontent with Aberdeen. Leila states that she wishes to educate readers about Islam and Muslim cultures through gentle claims about how problems between cultures arise "just because people don't know."[22] Reading fiction might make a difference, she suggests. Both the interviewer and the interviewee stay far from many of the more charged themes of *The Translator*, particularly the inherent critique of how the West engages with Islam and Muslims.

As *The Translator* gained a larger readership, Leila used a canonical and beloved English novel, Charlotte Brontë's *Jane Eyre*, to explain the romance between Sammar and Rae.[23] Despite Leila's persuasive pedagogical approaches to dispel misunderstandings about Islam and Muslims broadly, she would find that the Western world would repeatedly engage with her work either as some type of Muslim propaganda, or as an exotic window into an unknown universe.

Leila had been writing about Sudan and Africa for five years, but her work remained hemmed into a local Scottish sphere until her story "The Museum" suddenly found the spotlight.

The death of Sir Michael Harris Caine, head of the Booker food corporation, and a philanthropist who loved books, led to the creation of the first literary prize for a short story from Africa. Caine was a voracious reader and had "a lifelong interest in activities intended to encourage education in developing societies and foster greater understanding in Europe of third-world problems."[24] He was instrumental in the establishment of the Booker Prize in 1969, and he also headed organizations such as the Royal African Society, the Africa Centre, and the African Emerging Markets Fund among other Africa-centered economic and cultural institutions.[25]

The Caine Prize was founded with the aim of promoting African writing and expanding its audience. In its first year, the prize received entries from 20 African countries. Judges included Nigerian writer and 1991 Booker Prize winner Ben Okri, as the chair, writer Véronique Tadjo from Ivory Coast, British writer William Boyd, and American academic Alvaro Ribeiro.[26] All of the stories from Yvonne Vera's anthology *Opening Spaces* were submitted for the prize. Leila's "The Museum" was awarded the first Caine Prize in 2000. *The Guardian* ran a small blurb congratulating Leila and reported that she will "receive her $15,000 prize money this weekend in Harare to coincide with the Zimbabwe Book Fair."[27]

Winning the Caine Prize was a game changer. Even though it was the first-ever such prize, it put Leila on the radar of the right type of London literati, because of the prize's connections to the Booker, and to various prestigious African institutions. Even though writers like Abdulrazak Gurnah, J.M Coetzee, Ahdaf Soueif, and Buchi Emecheta, or editors such as Margaret Busby and Jason Cowley, were not as well-known at the time, they were all part of a small but growing clique of people who would influence the outcome of English-language, postcolonial writing.

The accolades were set in motion, and *The Translator* got longlisted for the Orange Prize for Fiction, awarded specifically to women writers. Though Leila did not make it to the shortlist, the titles chosen that year reflected the multicultural zeitgeist, and several of the nominated writers were exploring the theme of migration. This theme was so prevalent that it was confounding, as evidenced by an article about that year's long list published in *The Guardian*. Reporter John Ezard's article includes comments from that year's judges' chairperson, Polly Toynbee. "Stories of migration from one culture to another" were part of 9 out of 20 books, according to Toynbee, who noted that migration was a "tremendous wellspring for tension and imagination." Toynbee then adds: "After reading them all, you look at mothers begging with babies in their laps—Romanians or whatever—and you think, those kids are going to write a book someday."[28] Toynbee went on to become a rabid anti-Muslim commentator within the mainstream media.

These articles and such comments were an indicator of what Leila was up against, and how utterly offensive it was that a Muslim woman who practiced Islam and wore a headscarf should even dare penetrate a certain literary and cultural ethos.

Becoming less Sudanese

Somewhere in the middle of all the bustle, Leila gave birth to her third child, a girl named Manal, the "most expected baby." Leila remembers a big fuss over the pregnancy and over Manal's birth. Her oldest son Kareem's birth in 1986 was celebrated in Sudan, and she had left for the UK soon after. Their second son Ahmed was born in 1990 at a time when Leila and Nadir were still finding their bearings. Manal got lots of visitors and cards, and it was clear that the family had finally found genuine community in Aberdeen.

An inadvertent effect of Leila's plunge into Aberdeen life on an intellectual, social and public level as a writer was that she found herself "becoming less Sudanese." Until Aberdeen, Leila did not overly question her identity as a Muslim, but conflated it with being Sudanese, as something that was simply part of the cultural fabric of Sudanese-ness. She viewed herself as an "average" Muslim woman from Sudan, who did not question her own levels of religiosity nor ask how much effort she placed into the practice of her religion. But over time, she found that she began to identify more with British Muslims and the challenges they faced as a community. At Leila's Aberdeen mosque community, there was a shared concern about how to impart Muslim culture, languages, and values to their children. They would regularly hold open houses at the mosque and organize talks. Socializing with Sudanese people and engaging with the specificity of Sudanese culture started to take a back seat for Leila and her family. Even as connections with family remained strong with visits and phone calls, the feeling of not fitting into the UK had dissipated.

Aberdeen also began to infiltrate Leila's psyche as a place, and she started becoming attached to a few locations, many of which debut in *The Translator*, and appear again in *The Kindness of Enemies* and in *Bird Summons*. A connection to Aberdeen was encapsulated by an anecdote Leila liked to narrate about chancing upon the statue of Charles Gordon.[29] Gordon was an English general known for his steely determination for military conquest in the service of his beloved Britain. He was tasked with fighting the Mahdist army in 1885 in Sudan but was eventually killed in Khartoum. A statue of Gordon atop a camel, dressed in military uniform, was installed in Khartoum in 1905 but removed in 1958 after Sudan's independence from Britain. Gordon's statues are found in seven other locations in the UK and one in Australia.[30] Leila attended the University of Khartoum, which was previously named Gordon Memorial College; she was familiar with the mythology and iconography around Gordon.

Not particularly grand, Gordon's statue in Aberdeen is around the corner from the Aberdeen Central Library, which Leila frequented in her early days in the city. In an article detailing some of her favorite Aberdeen places, she explains: "I always had this connection to this statue, even before I came to Aberdeen and found the word 'Khartoum' on it, which had such an effect on me." In *The Translator*, Rae first mentions the statue to Sammar in order to offer her a connection, but Sammar is lost in her fog. Leila's desire to see a connection between Scotland and Sudan, albeit a colonial one, was reflected again in her novel *River Spirit,* about the Mahdist war.

In seeking locations for scenes for *The Translator*, Leila likely became closer to the city. The sprawling Winter Gardens housed the tropical plants section in Duthie Park, and Sammar and Rae's meeting among the tall cacti is the first symbolic meeting point between Scotland and Sudan. *The Translator* is a quintessential Aberdeen novel, with Sammar wandering, flanêur-like, in a dazed state from one location to another as she arrives for work at the cobblestone campus of the university or observes the shoppers and restaurant-goers on Union Street, one of the major commercial streets in the city.

Sammar's blurring of the boundaries between Khartoum and Aberdeen was a distinct stylistic element in Leila's early work. She explained in an interview:

> Walking in Aberdeen, stirring words about another place. Why not? Put homesickness into words, make sense of it, make stories of it, show the people around me that an African city, in one of the poorest countries in the world, is as atmospheric as London, livelier than Brighton, more beautiful than Edinburgh.[31]

Mapping Sudanese cityscapes and soundscapes onto Scottish ones shone the spotlight on two marginalized cities, Aberdeen and Khartoum.

In an autobiographical essay written in 1992, Leila revealed a depth of thinking on the topic of place and its connection to her writing. She admitted that Sudan, of course, remained a vibrant and lively presence in all her writing. But there was also this cold clarity: "If I go back to Sudan," she wrote, "I will never write again…[W]hen I went to Khartoum on holiday, the whizzing in my head stopped, there were no words in my head. I was, simply, too happy to write, too busy living to write about life."[32]

This whizzing, this churning could only be experienced far away from her beloved Sudan. Her connection and love for Sudan remained intact, but the grief and longing of previous years were gone, channeled into a literary tapestry. Leila felt fulfilled at the social, familial, and creative levels. Aberdeen had made that possible, and she felt resolute: "This is my new life. I'm here and I want to be a writer."

Notes

1 Leila Aboulela, "The Intrigue of the Image by Leila Aboulela," *Wasafiri*, March 30, 2023, https://www.wasafiri.org/content/the-intrigue-of-the-image-leila-aboulela/
2 Leila Aboulela, interview by Keija Parssinen.
3 Leila Aboulela, "Barbie in the Mosque," in *Being Scottish: Personal Reflections on Scottish Identity Today*, eds. Tom M. Devine and Paddy Logue (Edinburgh University Press: 2002), 1–3.
4 "What impact has the 1990 City of Culture had on Glasgow—30 years on?," *The Scotsman*, October 15, 2020, https://www.scotsman.com/heritage-and-retro/heritage/what-impact-has-the-1990-city-of-culture-had-on-glasgow-30-years-on-3000426
5 "Chapman Issue 82—Hamish Henderson's Long March," *Chapman: Scotland's Quality Literary Magazine*, https://www.chapman-pub.co.uk/magazine_details_082.php
6 "About Chapman," *Chapman*, https://www.chapman-pub.co.uk/about.php
7 "Hamish Henderson," *Scottish Poetry Library*. https://www.scottishpoetrylibrary.org.uk/poet/hamish-henderson/
8 Todd McEwen, "Left to Write," *Lemon Tree Writers*, November 26, 2016, https://lemontreewriters.wordpress.com/2016/11/26/left-to-write/
9 Leila Aboulela, "Missing Out," *Granta*, no. 111, July 12, 2010, https://granta.com/missing-out/
10 Leila Aboulela, *The Translator* (Grove Atlantic: 2006), 4.
11 Leila Aboulela, *The Translator* (Grove Atlantic: 2006), 22.
12 Leila Aboulela, *The Translator* (Grove Atlantic: 2006), 4.
13 Leila Aboulela, *The Translator* (Grove Atlantic: 2006), 74.
14 Leila Aboulela, *The Translator* (Grove Atlantic: 2006), 11.
15 Rashid, "Islamic Individualism and the Logic of the Narrative," 618.
16 Leila Aboulela, "The Museum," in *Elsewhere, Home* (Grove Atlantic: 2019), 158.
17 Leila Aboulela, "The Museum," in *Elsewhere, Home* (Grove Atlantic: 2019), 157.
18 Leila Aboulela, "The Museum," in *Elsewhere, Home* (Grove Atlantic: 2019), 182.
19 "Yvonne Vera," *African Books Collective*. https://www.africanbookscollective.com/authors-editors/yvonne-vera
20 Sharon Norris, "Failings of cross-cultural love and pin-striped Armageddon," *The Scotsman*, October 9, 1999, 10.
21 Carris O' Grady, "Fiction and Non-Fiction Paperbacks, Saturday Review, October 9," *The Guardian*, 1999, 55.
22 Susan Mansfield, "Profile: Bridging the Culture Gap," *Leisure, The Press and Journal* (Aberdeen), Saturday Dec 4, 13.
23 Leila Aboulela, "Writing as Spiritual Offering: A Conversation with Leila Aboulela," interview by Keija Parssinen, *World Literature Today*, vol. 94, no. 1 (Winter: 2020): 26–29.
24 Warren Hoge, "Sir Michael Caine, 71, Muse Behind Britain's Booker Prize," *New York Times*, March 24, 1999.
25 "Michael Harris Caine," *Wikipedia*, last edited on September 16, 2025, https://en.wikipedia.org/wiki/Michael_Harris_Caine
26 "Judges," *The Caine Prize for African Writing*, https://www.caineprize.com/previous-judges
27 From "The Loafer, Saturday Review," *The Guardian*, July 29, 2000, 10.

28 John Ezard, "Novelist sinks teeth into orange," National News, *The Guardian,* March 21, 2000, accessed on Apr 25, 2025, 5.
29 Eve Livingston, "My Aberdeen: Leila Aboulela," *hyphen*, September 22, 2022, https://hyphenonline.com/2022/09/22/my-aberdeen-leila-aboulela/
30 "Statue of General Gordon," *Wikipedia*, last edited on August 8, 2025, https://en.wikipedia.org/wiki/Statue_of_General_Gordon
31 Leila Aboulela, "Moving Away from Accuracy," *Alif: Journal of Comparative Poetics*, no. 22 (2002), 204.
32 Leila Aboulela, "Moving Away from Accuracy," *Alif: Journal of Comparative Poetics*, no. 22 (2002), 205.

6 Sudan Regained

A Homecoming

"I wrote without looking over my shoulder, bearing witness rather than feeding a demand."

Almost 30 years after Leila started writing and at the cusp of the publication of her sixth novel and eighth book, she reflected on the politics that have always undergirded her work. In an essay on her origins as a writer, Leila pondered the fact that she had been "capturing the movement of my own cohort of immigrants and their wider interconnections to the former British colonies." And this group mainly comprised Muslim women who "came from Iraq, Lebanon and, like me, from Sudan" in the 1990s. It was the only world she knew, but it was "unknown to many."

Soon enough, after the World Trade Center attacks of September 11, 2001, in New York City and the ensuing War on Terror that lasted two decades, this world had come to be perceived and described as the "Muslim Problem." But Leila had been cognizant of being perceived as a problem before 9/11. She was keenly aware of Islamophobia in the West, having already been writing about it without declarations of grand political intent. Inadvertently, she had been narrating the lives of the Muslim community in Britain, a particular angle that centered on the average adherent, rather than the rebels or the elites.[1]

Soon after *The Translator* was published, at the start of the new millennium, Nadir's career took Leila and their children to four cities: Jakarta, Dubai, Abu Dhabi, and Doha. The family moved back to Aberdeen in 2012.

Nested within these family journeys were individual journeys that could be seen as a series of homecomings for Leila. She had been absent from Sudan for 13 years. After that, she came home at every opportunity. These returns ignited her love for the country and its culture anew.

Returning to Aberdeen after 12 years in Asia and the Middle East constituted yet another homecoming. She was officially a successful writer

DOI: 10.4324/9781003306719-7

with international recognition. Over three decades later, Leila has gradually shed the pressures of the internalized voice of her own mother that always spurred a spiral of anxiety around ambition, achievement, and career. Mona and Leila's relationship had settled into a softer place. After her father Fuad died in 2008, Leila took on a caring role toward Mona. Leila herself was now the mother of three adult children and, like Mona, she had raised them while achieving a vibrant career. Likely surprising herself, Leila had become more like her mother than she had imagined. Her 2025 novella *A New Year* was ostensibly about a woman mourning the loss of her husband of 46 years, but in essence, it was a 128-page-long love letter to mothers.

***

Jakarta, Dubai, Abu Dhabi, and Doha (2000–2012)

For Leila and her family, the new millennium brought success, prosperity, and recognition. With the publication of *The Translator*, she secured her position in Scottish literary culture while also becoming part of the wider UK literary scene, having published in *Wasafiri* journal, the primary venue for international, postcolonial writers and Black diasporic writing in the UK. Her experimental prose poem "The Houriyah" was included in their special issue, "Taking the Cake: Black Writing in Britain," spearheaded by founding editor Susheila Nasta. Leila's poem was featured alongside weightier names like Stuart Hall, Kwame Dawes, Caryl Phillips, and Homi K. Bhabha.[2]

On the family front, Nadir had received an offer for an "expat" posting, and it came with the full suite of perks: higher salary, relocation allowance, big house, and fancy international schools for the children. However, this was in Jakarta, Indonesia, and thus far from the now-comfortable Aberdeen life that Leila had built for them.

Everything appeared to be changing for the better. It was a time of firsts. In late July of 2000, a month before the move to Jakarta, Leila was awarded the Caine Prize for African Writing, first in a ceremony at Oxford and then again in Harare, Zimbabwe. Leila, Nadir, and little Manal traveled from London to Harare, where Manal celebrated her second birthday. It was Leila's first trip to Southern Africa, and she felt at home in Harare, finding within it reminiscences of Khartoum.

On the trip, Leila met Zimbabwean writer Yvonne Vera, who had championed her work and submitted it to the prize. Vera described Leila as fearless, courageous, sensitive, and "for whom the world was just beginning to open up."[3] Leila recalls that Vera probably gave her "the best writing advice," which was simply that "the writer leads and the readers will always follow."

The visit to Harare was Leila's introduction to the burgeoning African literary world: the embrace by Vera, the humble pageantry of the Caine Prize, the sociality of a plane ride from London to Harare filled with the Caine shortlisted writers and the administrators, and the surprise that South African writer J.M. Coetzee had been at the prize ceremony, a fact she only realized the next morning. Even though Leila's reading included many postcolonial writers, she decided it was time to focus on African works: "I became very self-conscious that I have to read African books, and I hadn't because I was reading the Scottish books in Scotland...I systematically started to read African writers."

After her return from Harare, Leila received invitations to book festivals and commissions for stories and radio plays had multiplied. The Heinemann African Writers Series, which had previously declined to publish *The Translator,* now wanted to publish it in paperback with a new cover image. Whether viewed as an African writer, a Black British writer, or a Scottish writer, Leila was experiencing a hitherto unknown feeling of belonging. However, any sense of belonging was short-lived after the events of 9/11 and the ensuing War on Terror turned all Muslims into the enemy in the West.

The four years Leila spent in Jakarta were like a long writing residency. She was busy with various commissions including her BBC radio plays, and short stories for collections. She admits that she never really looked around, immersed in the city or developed a social life. "I was on a high with the writing and the reading. I read a lot because I had time. I had oodles of time...Weeks would go by and I just wouldn't leave the house."

A second novel was also brewing. Leila remembers writing the first few paragraphs of *Minaret* in a hotel as soon as they all landed in Jakarta, in 2000. Like *The Translator,* she wrote *Minaret* in fits and starts, often setting it aside to produce commissioned work. She worked on bringing together all her short stories in a collection which was published as *Coloured Lights* by Polygon Press in Edinburgh. Radio screenplays came easily for Leila, and the BBC had broadcast *Visitors, Cardamon, The Sea Warrior, The Translator, The Museum,* and *The Mystic Life* between 1999 and 2003. There was also the occasional travel with invitations to literary festivals and readings, which often meant putting *Minaret* aside.

September 11, 2001, came and went, without causing much upheaval in Jakarta. Perhaps because Indonesia was so far away from Europe and North America, and since it was also a majority Muslim country, Leila felt no palpable shift in their daily life. Yet there was an underlying anxiety. She was worried about her friends in Aberdeen, who told her the mosque had closed that day and that they had been asked to stay home. Her brother Khalid had moved to Canada, so she regularly checked in on him. In retrospect, Leila admits to feeling removed from the paranoia and its effects on the daily lives of Muslims, and feeling wrapped up in her career.

Unfortunately, the world had indeed become different for Muslims after 9/11, and Leila felt the first sting of this change when she went to Germany in 2002. *The Translator* had been translated into German, and she began to get questions about Osama Bin Laden during her book tour. She realized then that she did not have her ear to the ground. Having always written about being Muslim in the West, she was habituated to questions, even those bordering on microaggressions, about everything Muslim. But the overt hostility felt new. It took her by surprise.

Leila retreated to her Jakarta life, and even though she believes that the global resonances of 9/11 did not have an impact on *Minaret,* it is hard to imagine that she was able to shield herself from it entirely. Wars in Iraq and Afghanistan, illegal detentions at Guantanamo Bay and "extraordinary" renditions were already in the news. The victims were almost always Muslim, and several Muslim countries were also blacklisted. Sudan had been on this list since the early nineties, and the country now appeared more frequently in the media since it was the country where Bin Laden had lived and where he had grown much of his wealth.[4] Muslim women suddenly found themselves in the limelight as objects of Western savior ideologies, with the US invading Afghanistan under the pretext of saving women from the Taliban.[5]

Minaret soaked up much of this darkness in an unconscious way. To a degree, the fate of *Minaret's* protagonist, Najwa, is far more dire than that of Sammar. While *The Translator* moved from depression and tragedy toward self-realization and love, *Minaret* is the archetypal story of a fall from grace. Najwa rebuilds her life after losing wealth, status, and marriage prospects, the social capital that she was accustomed to, by turning inwards and finding peace in her faith. However, this is a far more cynical novel, and without the romantic ending of many of Leila's stories.

Najwa's trajectory of rejection is harsh, and the debasement and humiliation she continually suffers is different from Sammar, who retains confidence in her own views. It seems that Leila refused to protect Najwa from the reality of a racist and misogynistic world as she had done with Sammar, either through Rae in Scotland or through a return to the family unit in Khartoum. In a way, Leila's own disillusionment with how the world treats Muslim women seeped through the pages of her second book; they have no option but to turn inward, reaffirm, and lean on their faith to cope with a turbulent world.

Ironically, it was the cultural moment after 9/11 that led to the success of *Minaret* in sales and in international exposure. Curiosity about Muslim culture, whether well-intentioned or pernicious, was at an all-time high in the Anglophone world, and the success of Afghan American writer Khaled Hosseini's novel *The Kite Runner*, published in 2003, was an indicator of this trend. When it came to sales figures, published translations, bestseller lists, awards, and reviews, the numbers for *The Kite*

Runner were simply astounding: 21 million copies were sold in ten years, the novel remained on bestseller lists for 240 weeks,[6] and it was adapted into graphic novels, turned into theater productions, and made into a Hollywood film.

Minaret did not achieve the same level of monetary success as *The Kite Runner*, but the book's sales were high, especially for a relatively unknown, formerly Scotland-based writer who was also a writer from Sudan, a relatively unknown African country that did not garner the same mainstream attention in English-language literature as Nigeria or South Africa. As with *The Kite Runner*, a similar unhealthy fetish for an insider view into Muslim subjects drove much of the attention for the book and its author. A wider dissemination of the book meant Leila found herself in the bittersweet glare of the spotlight. *Minaret* was published by Bloomsbury, one of the biggest independent publishers in the UK, and simultaneously in the US by Grove Atlantic, yet another large, independent publisher. Following the success of *Minaret*, Grove Atlantic also published the American version of *The Translator* in 2006. This was the start of an important relationship that brought Leila's books to the substantial and important American market, and Grove Atlantic went on to publish the five books Leila has written since.

Homecoming: A time of fathers

Nadir's four years in Jakarta were up, and his next posting in the United Arab Emirates was transformative for Leila. The family lived in Dubai for one year, followed by four years in Abu Dhabi. Because it was much easier to fly from the UAE to Sudan than it had been from Aberdeen or Jakarta, Leila's world was within her reach. Not only was she close to Sudan, but she was also drawn into a literary scene that brought her close to her readers; the Muslim women who connected to her work, and for whom and about whom she had been writing. The self-motivated, focused writing mood that had marked her Jakarta years was over. Socialization, travel and festival appearances surged. Leila's readership had expanded significantly with *Minaret*, and the proof of its success became visible.

Leila returned to Sudan in 2005 after 13 years. Her first visit back was short, only one week. "But it broke the spell." After that, Leila kept going back for three weeks at a time and sometimes even longer. Her quintessential Sudan and the Khartoum she loved appeared unchanged to her. "When I returned to Sudan after being away, I continued to look for what was familiar, and it was still there, in patches, among the modernity and changes that had taken place over time."[7] And if there were crueler changes like echoes of a brutal war out west in Darfur or her childhood city eroded by years of a dictatorship, she refused to see it, and clung to her stubborn version of patriotism and nostalgia.

Leila socialized extensively during her visits to Sudan, and since *Minaret* was getting wide coverage and *The Translator* had been published in Arabic, there was also ceremony and celebration. Leila was treated with pride as the Sudanese writer who had achieved success and fame in the English-language world. It was a prodigal return. "I was very talked about in Sudan," Leila recalls giddily. "I was this wonderful writer and everybody loved me. And I just wanted to stay."

In a way, Leila did stay. She actively refreshed her Sudanese roots; her third novel, *Lyrics Alley*, was inspired by this homecoming and drew heavily from her family archive. As her returns grew more frequent, she pulled herself into the web of the extended Aboulela family, reconnecting with her Sudanese relatives, rebuilding relationships. She was older now; she was also successful, someone to be reckoned with. Importantly, she was returning after having her own nuclear family. Thus, her visits carried none of the school or college agendas associated with her mother, nor the tensions from when she lived in Khartoum and when she attended weekly family lunches in Omdurman as a young girl. This new Leila was free to submit to a version of a Sudanese-ness that she believed in.

In 2008 her father Fuad died of vascular dementia at 80. Fuad had become ill suddenly, and the disease advanced rapidly. He had remained obstinately settled in Khartoum, and Leila seemed to be re-entering his embrace in those few years before his death. In a moving essay published 12 years later, she recounts visiting the family grave with him in 2006 to pay her respects to all those who had died while she was abroad. The visit might have been somber, but Leila notes that

> my father had put up new curtains in the house, made sure all the light bulbs were working, spread new sheets on the beds. Throughout my childhood only important guests got this treatment. To my delight, I had become one of them.[8]

Lyrics Alley is a fictional account of her father's cousin, Hassan Awad Aboulela, whose tragic accident at the age of 19 left him a quadriplegic. He could not attend college, pursue the family business, or get married. Leila had always been open about how she drew material for her fiction from her own life. But in the author's note for *Lyrics Alley*, she was particularly honest:

> The crash of this dream traumatized my father, who was at the impressionable age of thirteen. And yet this was not the end of the story, for Fate twisted and held out a gift. The life of an invalid enabled Hassan

to develop his literary skills. In due course, he became not only an accomplished lyrical poet but a hugely successful one, as his verses were made into popular songs. His home became a literary salon, widening the family's social circle and influencing the younger members.[9]

Leila's use of the word "traumatized" to describe her own father's reaction, and the fact that Fuad was 13 years old at the time, was not lost on her. "My intention was to capture my father's childhood and youth and so I relied on his memories and perspective," Leila revealed in an interview, some years later.[10]

The research process for the novel also became a way for Leila to document the history of the vast family. As a child, Leila remembers that her mother felt a sense of alienation with the big Aboulela gatherings at the saraya and found them "difficult." Young Leila mimicked a disinterest in them as well, "out of loyalty" to her mother. Mona's Egyptian superiority imbued her with authority and meant that she didn't approve of traditional Sudanese family conventions, especially when it came to the different rules for men and women. But it all held a charm for Leila: "Even though I didn't follow the conventions and rules of my father's family, I still felt a lot of affection, I still saw it as beautiful."

Rescuing her Sudan from Egyptian criticism and Egyptian superiority was an impulse that became an obvious theme in *Lyrics Alley.* Set in the 1950s, the waning days of Anglo-Egyptian rule in Sudan, the novel builds Sudanese autonomy and independence from Egyptian influence into its world. In *Lyrics Alley,* the patriarch, Mahmoud, has a traditional Sudanese wife and a modern Egyptian wife, and he is often torn between their opposing perspectives on home and family life. Leila illustrates some of her own cultural, political, and psychological conflicts through this triangular structure in the novel. Despite attempts to craft a balanced representation of the two wives and thus the two nations, Egypt and Sudan, the novel ends in a divorce demanded by Nabilah, the Egyptian wife. Reconciliation, adaptation, and assimilation are not possible for Nabilah—but neither is it possible for Mahmoud, who chooses his large Sudanese family and remains committed to Sudan.

Many uncles and aunts are proud of Leila and speak fondly of the time she spent researching the Aboulela family for *Lyrics Alley.* However, their impressions of Leila as a young girl are fleeting. Almost unanimously, Leila is described as a quiet, timid girl who was very good at school and excelled in the English language. Her relatives, Awad Aboulela and his wife Abda Basheer, speak about Leila and her father being close, and are happy that she stayed connected to their side of the family: "She never forgot to be a Sudanese. She never gave up on being Sudanese." None had any inkling that she would become a writer. Ironically, they attribute her talent to being Egyptian. "The Egyptians are very good at storytelling," the couple insisted.

Leila definitively and impassionedly regained her Sudan, and on her own terms. All these years, Mona had been the towering presence in her life, and, unsurprisingly, mother figures had dominated her stories and books thus far. This became the time of fathers. Her attention to her father and her passion for Sudan were imbricated in the pages of *Lyrics Alley,* driven by the difficult and long absence from Sudan that had been mandated, to a large degree, by her Egyptian mother.

Split readerships and critical dissonance

The BBC continued to commission radio plays, usually on topics of Leila's own choosing. While in Jakarta, she completed a play called *The Lion of Chechnya,* inspired by an article she read on Imam Shamil in a Muslim publication. Shamil was one of the first known Muslim leaders who spent his life, almost the entirety of the 19th century, engaged in military resistance against imperial Russia. Leila had always wanted to turn the radio play into a novel, but it got pushed aside once *Lyrics Alley* became her focus.

Lyrics Alley had been completed and submitted to US and UK publishers by the time Leila and her family moved to Doha in 2009. Despite the revisions involved, Leila appreciated the fact that editors Arzu Tahsin in the UK and Elizabeth Schmitz in the US both "cared about" and "believed in" her third book. Given the success of *Minaret,* and with *Lyrics Alley* newly published, there was an effort to promote Leila into a rapidly growing multicultural literary scene that was exhibiting interest in African, Black, and postcolonial writers in Western cities. Her travel itinerary during these few years was extensive; it included the PEN World Voices Festival in New York, the Jaipur Literature Festival in India, events at prestigious venues such as the Harvard Bookstore in Cambridge, Massachusetts, as well as an invitation to Buckingham Palace.

Leila's oeuvre was becoming robust, which led to critical scrutiny of her work, especially in academia. Mainstream media outlets had focused on the themes of religiosity in her books and in her life, and academic articles developed these same themes, but the gavel came down much louder. They criticized her for the devoutly religious women characters and the foregrounding of Islam in all her work; those elements were seen as traditional, regressive, and orthodox. There were also narrow comparisons made with the other important and canonical Sudanese writer, Tayeb Salih, who wrote in Arabic.[11]

Leila was one of the first Sudanese women writers who published in English, and for Sudanese at home and abroad, she elicited pride for her Western laurels. *Lyrics Alley* had not yet come out but *The Translator,*

Minaret, and the short stories generated a split readership; an adoring fan base of English language readers in the Middle East and North Africa on the one hand, and a critical Western readership and scholarship that was ambivalent, at best, and rejecting, at worst, about her narratives of religious conversion and of women finding refuge in religion. For Western and Westernized readers, Leila's lack of rebellion against Islam, as typically expressed by Egyptian Nawal el Saadawi or Algerian Assia Djebar, was confounding and produced a sort of shame. It created dissonance and generated debate about whether her fiction espoused feminist values despite its rejection of secularist structures. Protagonists Sammar and Najwa were also seen as instruments for staging a critique of Marxist men, thus leading some leftist scholars to ask if her fiction was even politically progressive.[12]

In a way, writing in English and publishing in the West meant that Leila took on the role of an arbiter between her two readerships: the average reader who may need explanations when it comes to Islam, and those familiar with Muslim life, and thus could not be patronized or condescended to.

Even though the sales for *Lyrics Alley* were not as high as *Minaret,* it was a success, garnering praise, award nominations, and several reviews. Its world was also a completely different one, and it showed that Leila was able to weave a bigger tapestry that comprised elements of family saga, history, politics, and poetry. However, a major criticism of *Lyrics Alley* was that it projected a rosy and apolitical nostalgia where everyone, including the patriarchs and the colonials, is good, kind, and fair, and, of course, faith will make everything better, no matter the circumstances.[13]

The critiques were not unjustified, and indeed, *Lyrics Alley* emerged from a very particular phase of Leila's life; it over-expressed her patriotism to Sudan. But these ambivalences created by Leila's fiction also propelled it further, and by the time the second decade of the millennium dawned, her oeuvre seemed to surface everywhere and nowhere. It was accommodated into many trending literary categories, such as Arab, Muslim, Scottish, Sudanese, "halal" fiction,[14] and postcolonial fiction. But in a different arena, it was also seen as politically regressive and anti-secular and was not given much weight on university syllabi or within the realms of gender studies and women's writing.[15]

Pushing her own limits with a political novel

Leila read and followed everything that was written about her and was familiar with how she was perceived in different circles. But this did not make her deviate from her focus, nor did she try to bend her writing to satisfy critics. Even though Western validation, sales, and praise were welcome and necessary, her purpose was clear: she wrote for and about Muslims.

The Kindness of Enemies was her second historical novel. Set in the 19th century in the North Caucasus region, specifically Dagestan and Chechnya, during the time of Tsarist Russia's imperial incursions into Muslim territories, it was also her most overtly political novel. It was a piercing gaze into a historically meaningful past and was meant to shed light on the post-9/11 realities and challenges faced by Muslims in the West through the bookending narrative of history professor Natasha Wilson. The War on Terror loomed large in the public sphere, and concepts like "jihad" (a moral, political, and spiritual struggle) had become distorted in the media to become synonymous with terrorism. Leila plunged headlong into the topic of anti-colonial and revolutionary jihad itself by resurrecting the figure of Imam Shamil, one of the first known Muslim leaders engaged in military resistance against imperial Russia, the subject of her 2005 BBC radio play, *The Lions of Chechnya*.

Leila developed an innovative narrative structure to create a bridge between the past and the present: 19th-century Dagestan and Scotland in the year 2010. Natasha, the protagonist of the modern-day narrative, has a Sudanese father and a Russian mother. Her curiosity about her Sudanese and Muslim roots is folded into her research project about Shamil. This brings her in contact with Russian actress Malak and her son Osama (Oz), who is Natasha's student. They are also based in Scotland and are in possession of a sword belonging to Shamil. A snowstorm forces Natasha to spend a few days at Malak's farmhouse, prompting intellectual, political, and personal conversations about jihad, Islam, identity, family, and history, bringing the trio together over a couple of days.

The narrative about Shamil's efforts to lead Muslim groups to wars of resistance against Russia unfolds simultaneously. His eight-year-old son, Jamaledin, is captured by Russians and used as a bargaining chip by the Tsar to negotiate with Shamil. Shamil gains leverage by holding a Georgian princess, Anna, captive in hopes of a hostage exchange to get his son back. However, despite never fully belonging in Russia nor being accepted, Jamaledin becomes accustomed to his life in the Russian courts of St. Petersburg. His homecoming to Dagestan, 15 years later, is bittersweet; he finds that he does not fully belong in the land of his birth either. Jamaledin's identity crisis mirrors that of Natasha, who decides to return to Sudan to see and forgive her ailing father after 20 years, and reconcile the multiple cultural and religious strands of her identity.

After 12 years in Asia and the Middle East, Leila was back in Aberdeen. She got some of her writing focus back, but the first few years were not easy on the family, with Nadir somewhat unhappy at work and her children, especially Manal, finding Scotland to be a difficult adjustment. *The Kindness of Enemies* echoed some of these crises with its efforts to probe into questions of place, mobility and belonging, the impact of mixed marriages on children, the fragmentation of religious and cultural identity.

Leila had been grappling with these questions when she first moved to the UK. She had been part of organizing children's language and culture programs with the other members of the mosque. The challenge of raising children in the West while wanting to be committed to one's religion and heritage had always occupied Leila's mind. With her sons, Kareem and Ahmed, in their twenties, and Manal a teenager, she was able to analyze the varying effects of mixed marriages and multiple locations on different children.

Leila also found that Nadir and his brothers differed in terms of which culture they had each come to embrace: "When children come from these mixed marriages, each child has a different ingredient in them." Leila herself was, of course, a child of mixed marriage that pitted Sudan and Egypt against each other. In addition to these complex psychological dilemmas, the interlinked stories in *The Kindness of Enemies* explore the lives and challenges faced by Muslims in the Western world.

The *Kindness of Enemies* did not help bridge the gap around the debates that simultaneously saw her work as political and apolitical, regressive and progressive, and repressive or empowering. The novel's reception was muted; it was not reviewed much, nor did it get selected for prizes or awards. "The festivals continued. The invitations continued. It was the sales that dropped." To this day, Leila deems this to be a "turning point" with regard to sales because, commercially, sales of her books have yet to reach the same level achieved by *Minaret* and *Lyrics Alley.*

A second homecoming: Aberdeen (2012–2025)

By the time *The Kindness of Enemies* was published, Leila had entered her fifties. Life had resumed in Aberdeen, and Leila worked on a collection of short stories that included several older ones and some new ones. Titled *Elsewhere, Home,* the stories had begun to "reflect less of the culture-shocked protagonist and more of the global citizen," in Leila's own words.[16] She sensed a shift within herself—from the exilic melancholy that had defined her youth to settling into the consciousness of a confident, older woman. However, it was her next novel, *Bird Summons,* where this shift became more apparent.

Being back in Scotland and reviewing the many short stories she had written over two decades had revived many of Leila's previous preoccupations: mothers, journeys of faith, migration, and Muslim's women's interiority and self-reflexivity. But the narrative's reliance on one young female protagonist, like Sammar or Najwa, was gone.

In both her historical novels, Leila had created complex tableaus across space and time with a multiplicity of characters and narrators. *Bird Summons* retained some of that wide scope, even as it focused on a smaller, more compressed women's unit. Three women of different ages embark on a road trip across the Scottish Highlands. Two of the main characters, Salma and Moni, are at different stages of middle age and are reflecting on their marriages, motherhood, and careers. Salma is a massage therapist who had aspired to become a doctor but had failed her qualifying exams upon arrival in Britain from Egypt. Comfortably married and with three children, Salma is the matriarch who organizes the road trip and indulges in "dreams of a parallel life," the most significant among them being an online flirtation with ex-boyfriend Amir who still lives in Egypt.[17]

Sudanese migrant Moni's burden is her son Adam, who suffers from cerebral palsy. Having a child born with a severe disability puts a strain on her marriage and career, and even as motherhood becomes her first duty, she becomes aware that everything else is slipping away. The third protagonist of Kurdish Syrian descent, Iman, is young and beautiful. She has no job nor any idea how to earn an income; she is becoming too dependent on the many unreliable men she attaches herself to.

This motley crew of women of three ages, nationalities, and personalities has met at the Arabic-Speaking Muslim Women's Group. They have decided to locate the grave of Lady Evelyn Cobbold, a convert to Islam and one of the first British women to go on a pilgrimage to Mecca. The official plan is "to educate themselves about the history of Islam in Britain…those for whom this island was an inherited rather than adopted home."[18] But the trip is also a welcome break for three women coping with stress and pondering the meanings of their lives more broadly.

The enlargement of the compressed story comes in the form of a surrealist motif inspired by a combination of ancient Islamic fables, Christian allegory, and Scottish folktales. When the women arrive at a monastery adjacent to the Lady Evelyn's grave, they are visited by the Hoopoe—a bird that symbolizes wisdom and spiritual guidance in *The Conference of the Birds,* a 12th-century poem by Farid ud-Din Attar, a Persian poet and scholar of Sufism. The Hoopoe appears to all three women, who go on to have hallucinatory experiences where they are unable to distinguish dream from reality. The mythical engages them on an intellectual, spiritual, and intimate level, allowing them to come off the precipices of indecision and make morally sound choices. Thus, a potential fun trip away becomes a transformative journey.

Bird Summons gives the impression of being a departure from Leila's previous work because of the elements of speculative fiction, and is formally different and experimental. At its core, however, it is a more profound exploration of questions that have always plagued her: Where is home? How can the deepening of faith bring about spiritual, psychological, and moral growth? Can women find freedom and autonomy while straddling the obligations of marriage and motherhood? Do women need men? *Bird Summons* was a bold foray into a more mystical realm, where Leila attempted to decisively resolve these questions.

Without a shred of doubt, and just as with previous works, Leila reaffirmed the deepening of faith as the only way forward, the only solution. But these characters neither experienced nor tolerated debasement and humiliation; they arrived within the story as fully formed and empowered women. Even as Salma, Moni and Iman did not profess to fully belong in Scotland, they did not suffer from pangs of homesickness either. Leila had turned the page on the topic of migration. Of course, home was still an elusive concept, and homesickness never entirely disappeared—but returning to the country of one's birth was not the remedy either. If it had been implied in the previous novels, then *Bird Summons* declared it resoundingly: home, refuge, belonging, and identity were within us. These were internal journeys that could be traversed and resolved through faith.

Leila's return to Scotland in her fiction had a new, unencumbered quality. In *The Kindness of Enemies,* Leila's prose evocatively captured the rugged and mountainous terrain of Dagestan while juxtaposing it with the wooded, snowy landscapes of Scotland. In *Bird Summons,* nature descriptions of the journey through the Scottish Highlands, and the time spent by the ladies at the resort on the loch are evoked in tones of admiration and pleasure, rather than to signal melancholy or tumult as with previous novels.

This unencumbered quality would appear in Leila's writing on Sudan as well, evident in her next novel, *River Spirit,* another historical novel about Sudan, but without the obvious and overwrought nostalgia of *Lyrics Alley.*

River Spirit dived into weightier themes like war and slavery and did not shy away from the depiction of physical violence. Set in the late 19th century, it explored a particularly fraught moment for Sudan as the Mahdist wars attempted to stave off Egyptian and British colonialism. The women characters in *River Spirit* are even more empowered, fierce, and decisive. The novel opens with a Shilluk woman warrior, Rabiha, armed with a spear, as she bounds across the forest at night to warn the Mahdi of an impending attack. The protagonist, Akuany, is a Black girl from the tribes by the Nile River. Kidnapped at a young age and sold as a slave to various Arab families, she eventually catches the eye of a Scottish engineer and painter, Robert, who purchases her in order to paint her. She is made to sit still, tied to a chair, and dragged around in different positions so that Robert can capture her in the way he deems aesthetic.

Akuany resists and refuses: "He disgusted her with his poking and examinations, his insistence on paralyzing her on canvas. In response, she would glare at his paintings, cursing them. Her curses, melodious and repetitive, unnerved him, and that filled her with satisfaction."[19] She is so inflamed by seeing her private self on Robert's canvas that "she took a knife from the kitchen and slashed the painting."[20] Akuany's fiery spirit, her unchecked anger, and violent modes of resistance make her a very different kind of woman character in Leila's fiction.

Additionally, a cast of resilient and resourceful women characters—Fatima, Salha and Halima—ensure that *River Spirit* is a novel anchored in a world of strong women who are unlikely to be mentioned even in the footnotes of history. Even as important men rage away—waging wars, toppling governments and inscribing themselves into military histories—it is women who are the life force, and it is they who will rebuild and revive post-war Sudan.

Sudan, mothers, and faith: A triptych

In her three-decades journey as a writer, Leila was shaped by three intensely powerful forces that are a perennial source of pain but have also propelled her success: leaving Sudan but capturing it in her fiction; the simultaneously anchoring and unmooring influence of her mother, Mona; and her relationship to and defense of Islam.

Leila's coming of age as an artist begins with the loss of her beloved Sudan. The move to the UK had felt temporary, but once she realized that she would never going to return to Khartoum, the imagined vision of her future collapsed. And it broke her heart. It is this grief and loss that she channeled into her writing as she honed the bittersweet experience of exile into a craft.

Through the worldmaking exercise of her fiction, Leila has recreated and preserved her lost home of (Sudan), and this is the first component that marks her ascendancy and cements her reputation as a Sudanese writer of migration. Yet, her connection to Sudan is not static, and her fiction reflects an emotionally and intellectually evolving relationship with the country. Even so, perhaps home is elsewhere—as the title of her story collection suggests—and remaking and rebuilding after having departed from one's home is a necessary process. Leila's embrace of Scotland and making it into a home are vital parts of her personal and artistic journey. In her fiction, she moves from depicting it as unbearably gloomy in the early days to a vivid, inspiring, and spiritually generative place.

After a long absence, Leila returned and reclaimed Sudan. She has explored Sudan as a space of longing and loss, as a political place gaining independence from Egypt, and as an important historical site where an anti-colonial uprising took place. Additionally, as a Sudanese writer who writes from Scotland and detects Sudan's links to Scottish history, she found a peculiar and unique niche in the Anglophone literary world.

If Sudan is part of Leila's coming-of-age arc, then Mona, her mother, can be seen as her origin story. Leila's relationship with her mother and the enduring, powerful impact it has had on her as a person and as a writer cannot be underestimated. From the very beginning, Leila has found herself in a double bond with her mother. The first iteration of this bond is in the form of a dependency born of love, respect, and trust that only her mother knew what was best for Leila. Leila's dedication to her mother was and is absolute.

The flip side of this bond evokes the act of being forcibly tied up, imprisoned in a particular mother-daughter dynamic. For many years, Leila only knew herself as how she was reflected in her mother's eyes. In that sense, Mona shaped Leila's educational journey with a rigid, heavy-handed intensity until Leila was not invited to join a PhD program in statistics, an event completely out of Mona's control. With Mona managing her own career after Egyptian academics were expelled from Sudan, she had no time and energy to re-engage, lead, and steer Leila back onto the doctoral path. Strangely, suddenly, Mona let go.

And despite an overwhelming sense of her mother's disappointment echoing inside her head, Leila grabbed this opening, and found herself on a hitherto unimagined, wayward path: storytelling. But it was precisely making up stories and the freeing process of writing that allowed Leila to navigate the overpowering and intense influence of her mother. The exploration of mother figures and complex women, broadly, is the wellspring of Leila's creativity. It also drives Leila's readership since there is no doubt that Leila is a quintessentially woman-centric writer. Even when she makes forays into writing about men, it is always the women that come alive in her fiction. It can be argued that her understanding of women, as well as of women's friendships and relationships, in her fiction can be attributed to her complex bond with her mother.

Here too, Leila has come a long way. Her early stories and novels depicted crudely asymmetrical relationships between diminutive daughters and dominating matriarchs. But the daughters changed over time and became bolder and more self-realized. As the women in Leila's fiction got older, they gained autonomy and located their own reservoirs of inner strength. In her personal life, it would be far-fetched to say that Leila had completely shed her mother's overwhelming influence, but she had certainly arrived at a comfortable, safe place with her mother. Perhaps becoming a mother herself, finding her own version of career success, and working through the relationship within her fiction were important factors in that journey. Leila admits that even now, at 80 years of age, Mona mentions the PhD debacle from the early nineties and "blames herself" for not pushing Leila to pursue a doctorate, after all.

Leila's response to her mother digging up these old issues is revealing. Rather than feel reprimanded, she placates her mother. She reminds Mona that she was living far away from her husband, and that he was not enthusiastically backing her plans for their daughter. "For her to singlehandedly push me, my family, my husband and two children into me doing a PhD was too much. It was too much for her to do."

When it came to mothers, a new, resolved and more tender approach was once again reflected in her fiction. Leila published a novella titled

A New Year in 2025. In the novella, protagonist Suad has been recently widowed and is mourning the loss of Sherif, her husband of 46 years. Not wanting to live all by herself, she takes turns staying with each of her three children, all of whom are well into adulthood and have children of their own.

Suad is unable to integrate herself into their lives and feels unwanted and not needed as a mother. But some of the grief has ebbed from having spent time away, and she returns to her own home in London determined to remake life without her husband. Her children and grandchildren visit her for the new year on Eid, and the story ends on a warm note of a loving family reunion. In a review, Sadia Zulfiqar accurately points out that, "Suad finds her peace not by chasing motherhood, but by returning to the home she shared with Sherif. Her children still love her, undoubtedly, but they also love other people and other things. Love remains—but its intensity and relevance have changed."[21]

The final and, perhaps, the main motivating and driving force in Leila's life is Islam; not only with regards to the peace, freedom, solace, and beauty she finds in it, but also in the agonizing role of having to defend Islam in an anti-Muslim West. Within this spectrum of prejudice, Muslim women are particular targets of hatred, abuse, and extreme forms of misinterpretation. Leila has been open about her own religious journey: she chose to mark herself as Muslim by donning a head covering upon moving to the UK. This was in defiance of her father and her circle of bourgeois Khartoum society, and the strictly Christian and Western cultural norms in London and then in Aberdeen. Her first two novels and the early short stories explore how women needed their religion if they had to survive hostile, Islamophobic places, and Islam is shown as their only path toward self-realization.

Leila's Muslim woman is modern, with an embattled yet fully fleshed-out interior life that is simultaneously psychological, spiritual, and emancipatory. Her novels upend typical and often racist characterizations of Muslim women within liberal mainstream discourses as oppressed by their religion and lacking any autonomy over their own lives. Many of her women protagonists turn to an individualized and often spiritual strand of Islam to cope with past traumas, migrant alienation, failed love stories, depression, and to gain control over cultural constrictions. These women find breathing room in Leila's narratives, which bypass the binary of oppressed and empowered.

In her later novels, some of the insistence that Islam is the only way forward fell away, but the religion itself is infused in all her books: scenes of prayer abound; characters reflect on their problems by engaging with quotations from the Quran; there are references to other Muslim texts; religious debates are staged between characters; and the mosque is a key setting. Her novels, especially the more openly political ones, arrived within a fraught post-9/11 period with unprecedented levels of violence against the larger Arab and Muslim world with the War on Terror, the *longue durée* wars in Iraq and Afghanistan, the innumerable incarceration and surveillance projects that scapegoat Muslim men, and the amplification of saviorist rhetoric around Muslim women. This is the broad and disconcerting context within which Leila continues to mount a stubborn, feminist, and politically charged defense of Islam and specifically, Muslim women.

Despite her enormous success as a writer, not having pursued the PhD in statistics had always nagged at Leila, and Mona's preoccupation with that moment from almost 30 years ago meant that the wound was never allowed to close. In 2024, Leila enrolled in a PhD program in Creative Writing at the University of Aberdeen. She had decided to give academia yet another shot, but this time it was on her own terms; she had chosen to approach a field she had already mastered but through a different prism.

Mona, now settled in Canada in a small town outside of Toronto, only a few minutes away from her son Khalid and his family, is ecstatic about Leila's journey to a doctorate. Leila is amused by her mother's pride and makes fun of herself for finishing what she started decades ago only after having turned 60 years old.

Always someone who enjoyed assigned and structured reading, Leila now ventures happily into dense tomes of literary criticism and theory to write her doctoral dissertation titled "Muslim Spiritual Sensibility in Fiction: Positioning Bird Summons in the Secular Literary Marketplace."

The literary world takes note

In the year 2025, the literary world took note of Leila's longstanding commitment to migrant Muslim women. She was awarded the PEN Pinter Prize given by English PEN to writers who show "fierce intellectual determination" and an attempt "to define the real truth of our lives and our societies." With parallel devastating wars in Palestine and in Sudan, and a surge in anti-Muslim hatred, Leila's work is urgent and relevant. Chair of English PEN and judge Ruth Borthwick called her "a writer for this moment." She added: "In a world seemingly on fire, and with immense suffering unmarked and little mourned in Sudan, Gaza, and beyond, her writing is a balm, a shelter, and an inspiration." Co-judge and Somali British writer Nadifa Mohammed stated that Leila's work "is marked by a commitment to make the lives and decisions of Muslim women central to her fiction, and to examine their struggles and pleasures with dignity."[22]

Leila told *The Guardian* that the prize was "a complete and utter surprise." This response was indicative of her own awareness of the ways in which her work has been pigeonholed, and of the knowledge that such honors are usually reserved for Muslim writers whose works espouse a critique of Islam through an embrace of Western liberal ideals. Leila explained that the prize "brings expansion and depth to the meaning of freedom of expression and whose stories get heard," and "as a Muslim Sudanese immigrant who writes from a religious perspective probing the limits of secular tolerance, this recognition feels truly significant."[23]

Leila was awarded the prize on October 10, 2025, in a modest ceremony held at the British Library in London. Tall and commanding, Leila had chosen to wear a navy-blue Sudanese tobe patterned with glittering, floral embroidery. This was her nod to Sudan, and the now three-year war that had led to the fall of Khartoum was front and center. She delivered a 20-minute address that synthesized some of the elements from her

Figure 6.1 Leila at the PEN Pinter Prize ceremony, London, October 10, 2025

doctoral work. She began with the heartache she felt for the devastation in Sudan and in Palestine and moved to her lifelong object of study and creativity: the misrepresentation of Muslims in the West.[24]

"Islamophobia poses as a mirror that reflects the truth about Muslims, but it is inaccurate," Leila declared. Borrowing from Edward Said, she said that "malicious generalizations about Islam have become the last acceptable form of denigration of foreign culture in the West."[25]

Leila's speech, though delivered in a timid style, was deeply resistant, and made a case for the Islamic inner logic and story worlds of her fiction. But characteristic of Leila, it was neither adversarial nor politically belligerent: "Fortunately, I have found that fiction can open conversations rather than shut them down. I have found that by writing novels, I could invite readers to a more nuanced understanding of Islam and the religious experience."

At the core of this speech was a heartfelt invitation. Just as she had done for three decades, it was a simple plea to the Western world to put aside prejudices and differences about Islam. And Leila continues to build this bridge by immersing us in the stories and journeys of Muslims.

Notes

1 Leila Aboulela, "The Intrigue of the Image," *Wasafiri*, March 30, 2023, https://www.wasafiri.org/content/the-intrigue-of-the-image-leila-aboulela/
2 Susheila Nasta, ed., "Taking the Cake: Black Writing in Britain," special issue, *Wasafiri*, no. 29 (Spring 1999), https://www.wasafiri.org/issues/wasafiri-issue-29/
3 Helon Habila, "Obituary: Yvonne Vera," *The Guardian*, April 27, 2005, https://www.theguardian.com/news/2005/apr/27/guardianobituaries.books
4 Van Horne and Sheryl L., "Sudan Expels Osama Bin Laden," *EBSCO*, 2023, https://www.ebsco.com/research-starters/diplomacy-and-international-relations/sudan-expels-osama-bin-laden
5 Lila Abu-Lughod, *Do Muslim Women Need Saving?* (Harvard University Press: 2013).
6 "Book Facts," *Khaled Hosseini*, https://khaledhosseini.com/book-facts/
7 Leila Aboulela, "Perspectives of a Literary Artist," interview by *500 Words Magazine*, April 10, 2014, https://500wordsmag.com/interviews/exclusive-interview-leila-aboulela-perspectives-of-a-literary-artist/
8 Aboulela, "A Mention of My Father."Leila Aboulela, "A Mention of My Father," in *Elsewhere, Home* (Grove Atlantic: 2019).
9 Leila Aboulela, "Why I Wrote... Lyrics Alley," *Lyrics Alley*, https://leila-aboulela.com/books/lyrics-alley/
10 Leila Aboulela, "Exclusive Interview: Leila Aboulela – Perspectives of a Literary Artist," interview, *500 Words Magazine*, April 10, 2014.
11 Waïl S. Hassan, "Leila Aboulela and the Ideology of Muslim Immigrant Fiction." *Novel: A Forum om Fiction*. Vol. 41, No. 2/3, The Form of Postcolonial African Fiction (Spring - Summer, 2008), pp. 298–319 and Eiman Abbas Hassan El-Nour, "Forward to the past: Generational regression in Sudanese women's fiction." *The Ahfad Journal: Women and Change*; Omdurman, vol. 34, no. 1, (Jun 2017): 23–28.

12 Sadia Abbas, "Leila Aboulela, Religion, and the Challenge of the Novel." *Contemporary Literature*, vol. 52, no. 3, fall 2011, 430–461.
13 M. Lynx Qualey, "Lyrics Alley by Leila Aboulela – Review," *The Guardian*, April 8, 2011; Robin Yassin-Kassab, "Review: Lyrics Alley by Leila Aboulela," *Wasafiri*, January 17, 2015; Eva Hunter, "The Muslim 'Who Has Faith' in Leila Aboulela's Novels Minaret (2005) and Lyrics Alley (2009)," *Current Writing: Text and Reception in Southern Africa*, vol. 25, no. 1, 2013, 88–89.
14 Peter Morey, "'Halal fiction' and the limits of postsecularism: Criticism, critique, and the Muslim in Leila Aboulela's Minaret," *The Journal of Commonwealth Literature*, vol. 53, no. 2, 2018, 301–315.
15 Lily Saint and Bhakti Shringarpure, "African literature is a country," *Africa is a Country*, August, 2020. https://africasacountry.com/2020/08/african-literature-is-a-country
16 Leila Aboulela, *Bird Summons* (Black Cat: 2023), 16.
17 Leila Aboulela, *Bird Summons* (Black Cat: 2023), 15.
18 Leila Aboulela, *Bird Summons* (Black Cat: 2023), 1.
19 Leila Aboulela, *River Spirit* (Grove Atlantic: 2023), 198.
20 Leila Aboulela, *River Spirit* (Grove Atlantic: 2023), 199.
21 Sadia Zulfiqar, "Fiction: The Process of Grief," *Dawn*, August 17, 2025, https://www.dawn.com/news/1931440
22 Ella Creamer, "Leila Aboulela wins PEN Pinter prize for writing on migration and faith," *The Guardian*, July 9, 2025, https://www.theguardian.com/books/2025/jul/09/leila-aboulela-wins-pen-pinter-prize-sudanese-writer-muslim-women
23 Ella Creamer, "Leila Aboulela wins PEN Pinter prize for writing on migration and faith," *The Guardian*, July 9, 2025, https://www.theguardian.com/books/2025/jul/09/leila-aboulela-wins-pen-pinter-prize-sudanese-writer-muslim-women
24 Observations based on my attendance at the ceremony held at Pigotte Theater, British Library, October 10, 2025; "Leila Aboulela shares PEN Pinter Prize 2025 with Stella Gaitano," *English Pen*, October 10, 2025, https://www.englishpen.org/posts/campaigns/leila-aboulela-shares-pen-pinter-prize-2025-with-stella-gaitano/
25 Ella Creamer, "Leila Aboulela Wins PEN Pinter Prize for Writing on Migration and Faith," *The Guardian*, July 9, 2025.

Acknowledgments

This book owes everything to its subject: Leila Aboulela. I am thankful to Leila, not only for being an inspiration but also for letting me in, for sitting down with me for long conversations in her home in Aberdeen and online, for walking me through the beautifully preserved family albums, and for allowing me to speak with her family members and friends. Much gratitude also to the patient and generous people in Leila's life who welcomed conversations with me: Mona Khalifa in Toronto, Nadir Mahjoub in Aberdeen, Muhammad Awad, Abda Basheer, Hanan Talat, Fatma Izzedin and Sara Abdelaziz in Khartoum, and Todd McEwan in Edinburgh.

A very special thank you to the energetic, vibrant, sharp, and charming Mona Khalifa who met me for two very long sessions in Toronto.

A special thank you to Abda Basheer for taking me all over Khartoum and Omdurman, showing me the old family homes as well as the grand saraya, the Mahdi's tomb, and the downtown Aboulela office complex. It was a difficult day because Khartoum and Omdurman had been plunged into mourning for the brave, young protesters who had been martyred the day before, and Abda was a sympathetic guide and patient educator.

Another special thank you to Sara Abdelaziz who drove me around Al-Amarat as we hopped and peered over walls to find her old friend Leila's home, and for the sweet glimpses into their shared Khartoum girlhood.

The book's research and writing would not have been possible without the privilege of two incredible fellowships. First, at the Institute of Advanced Studies in the Humanities at the University of Edinburgh in Scotland. Second, at The Stellenbosch Institute of Advanced Studies in South Africa. Something about the open beauty of Edinburgh and Stellenbosch helped me connect more to Leila's writing and made my own writing process joyful and pleasurable. Thank you also to Helena Hurd at Routledge for her dedication and commitment to bringing the African writers' biography series to life.

It is a daunting task to construct a life, especially when there is a strict word length. And it takes a village. Thank you to Lily Saint for embarking on our African writers' lives journey together, and for the intellect, rigor, and friendship that you bring to it. Love, admiration, and gratitude to Madhuri Sastry for being the book's editor, and for becoming the first and vital interlocutor for it; for your brilliant psychological and literary insights, for taking pleasure in it, and, of course, for your keen editing. Appreciation and gratitude to Tom Recchio, for being a fast and clever copy editor, for bringing this book down to size, and for your wisdom and encouraging words.

Thank you to early readers Sherry Zane, Greg Pierrot, Suchitra Vijayan, and Eleni Coundouriotis, for your time, your comments, and your encouragement. Much appreciation to those who were present, positive, and complimentary along the way whether as listeners of talks, as readers of excerpts, as brainstormers, as helpers, as cheerleaders: Ainehi Edoro, Carli Coetzee, Alexandra Moore, Tina Steiner, Veruska Cantelli, Sadia Zulfiqar, Farah Baakari and Aruni Kashyap. Extra love and gratitude to Mustapha and Meg, for offering much-needed connection, and for intellectually and emotionally indulging the doom and gloom in our end times.

It is not clear to me how this book kept writing itself, perhaps it became a strange little oasis as worlds kept vanishing before my eyes in the last three years. My academic career was undone by the University of Connecticut, and along with that, my home and life there, and they also destroyed my dear Sherry. Revenge is on its way.

Soon came the devastation in Sudan and the cannibalization of Palestine. Through cycles of grief, mourning, and rage, Michael is my truest companion. For embracing the madness of building new worlds with me, and for his mind, his tireless support, his love. Deepest thank you. Loves of my life, Surya and Nour who are so clever, empathetic, courageous, and always in my corner. They make me proud; they keep my heart beating.

Unpublished Source Material

Interviews

- Interview with Leila Aboulela, Online/Zoom, July 22, 2024.
- Interview with Leila Aboulela, in-person, Aberdeen, November 9, 2021.
- Interview with Leila Aboulela, in-person, Aberdeen, September 8, 2022.
- Interview with Leila Aboulela, Online/Zoom, April 7, 2021.
- Interview with Nadir Mahjoub (husband), in-person, Aberdeen, September 8, 2022.
- Interview with Mona Khalifa (mother), in-person, Toronto, May 4–5, 2022.
- Interview with Sarah Abdelaziz (school friend), in-person, Khartoum, July 8, 2022.
- Interview (joint) with Awad Aboulela and Abda Basheer (relatives), in-person, Khartoum, July 2, 2022.
- Interview with Todd McEwan (mentor and professor), in-person, Edinburgh, November 7, 2022.
- Email correspondence: 14 email threads with Leila Aboulela from June 25, 2022–December 5, 2025.
- Leila Aboulela, "America, Owner of the Moon," unpublished draft. Written in November 2004.

Selected Bibliography

Abbas, Ali A. "Notes on Tayeb Salih: 'Season of Migration to the North' and 'The Wedding of Zein'," *Sudan Notes and Records* 55, (1974): 46–60.

Abbas, Sadia. "Leila Aboulela, Religion, and the Challenge of the Novel." *Contemporary Literature* 52, no. 3 (2011): 430–461.

Aboulela, Leila. "Baby love." *Wasafiri* 19, no. 42 (2004): 121–24. https://doi.org/10.1080/02690050408589926

Aboulela, Leila. *Bird Summons.* Black Cat, 2023.

Aboulela, Leila. *Coloured Lights.* Polygon, 2001.

Aboulela, Leila. "Farida's Eyes." In *Elsewhere, Home.* Black Cat, 2019.

Aboulela, Leila. "A Mention of My Father." *Jalada Africa*, no. 09 (Nostalgia) (2020). https://jaladaafrica.org/2020/12/04/a-mention-of-my-father-by-leila-aboulela/

Aboulela, Leila. "Moving Away from Accuracy." *Alif: Journal of Comparative Politics*, no. 22 (2002): 198–207.

Aboulela, Leila. *Lyrics Alley.* Orion Books, 2010.

Aboulela, Leila. *Minaret.* Grove Atlantic, 2005.

Aboulela, Leila. *River Spirit.* Grove Atlantic, 2023.

Aboulela, Leila. *The Translator.* Grove Atlantic, 2006.

Abu-Lughod, Lila. *Do Muslim Women Need Saving?* Harvard University Press, 2013.

Armstrong, Nancy. *Desire and Domestic Fiction: A Political History of the Novel.* Oxford University Press, 1990.

Bourne, Jenny. "'May we bring harmony'? Thatcher's legacy on 'race.'" *Race & Class* 55, no. 1 (2013): 87–91. https://doi.org/10.1177/0306396813489247

Collins, Robert O. *A History of Modern Sudan.* Cambridge University Press, 2008.

El-Nour, Eiman Abbas Hassan. "Forward to the past: Generational regression in Sudanese women's fiction." *The Ahfad Journal: Women and Change* 34, no. 1 (2017): 23–28.

Hassan, Waïl S. "Leila Aboulela and the Ideology of Muslim Immigrant Fiction." *Novel: A Forum on Fiction* 41, no. 2/3 (2008): 298–319.

Hunter, Eva. "The Muslim 'Who Has Faith' in Leila Aboulela's Novels Minaret (2005) and Lyrics Alley (2009)." *Current Writing: Text and Reception in Southern Africa* 25, no. 1 (2013): 88–89.

Mahjoub, Jamal. "Salamanca." *Transition* 13, no. 3 (2007): 138–147.

Morey, Peter. "'Halal fiction' and the limits of postsecularism: Criticism, critique, and the Muslim in Leila Aboulela's Minaret." *The Journal of Commonwealth Literature* 53, no. 2 (2018): 301–315.

Nelson, Harold D. *Sudan: A Country Study*. US Govt. 3rd edition. Print Office, 1982. https://catalog.hathitrust.org/Record/001544141

O'Connell, Lisa. *The Origins of the English Marriage Plot: Literature, Politics and Religion in the Eighteenth Century*. Cambridge University Press, 2019.

Osman, Safa Mohammed Kheir. "Sudanese Women's Participation in the December 2018 Revolution: Historical Roots and Mobilisation Patterns." *Ordinary Sudan 1504–2019: From Social History to Politics from Below Volume 1*. Edited by Elena Vezzadini, Iris Seri-Hersch, Lucie Revilla, Anaël Poussier and Mahassin Abdul Jalil. De Gruyter, 2023, 57–86.

Rashid, C.E. "Islamic Individualism and the Logic of the Narrative: An Interview with Leila Aboulela." *Interventions* 14, no. 4 (2012): 613–624. https://doi.org/10.1080/1369801X.2012.730863

Said, Edward. *Out of Place: A Memoir*. Alfred Knopf, 1996.

Salih, Tayeb. *The Wedding of Zein*. Translated by Denys Johnson-Davies. Three Continents Press, 1968.

Silvera, Alain. "Victoria College." In *Encyclopedia of the Modern Middle East and North Africa*. Macmillan Reference USA, 2004.

Steiner, Tina. "Strategic nostalgia, Islam and cultural translation in Leila Aboulela's The Translator and Coloured Lights." *Current Writing: Text and Reception in Southern Africa* 20, no. 2 (2008): 7–25.

"The Sennar Dam and the Gezira Irrigation Project." *Nature* 117 (1926): 200–201.

Vezzadini, Elena. "Emancipation through the Press: The Women's Movement and its Discourses on the 'Women's Problem' in Sudan on the Eve of Independence (1950–1956)." *Ordinary Sudan, 1504–2019: From Social History to Politics from Below Volume 1*. Edited by Elena Vezzadini, Iris Seri-Hersch, Lucie Revilla, Anaël Poussier and Mahassin Abdul Jalil. De Gruyter, 2023, 147–178.

Index

www.ingramcontent.com/pod-product-compliance
Lightning Source LLC
LaVergne TN
LVHW012002040926
847296LV00029B/311
* 9 7 8 1 0 3 2 3 0 7 9 9 2 *